Norman Geras

London: NLB
Atlantic Highlands: Humanities Press

The Legacy of
Rosa Luxemburg

ISBN 902308 28 9
First published 1976
© NLB 1976
NLB, 7 Carlisle Street, London W1
Printed in Great Britain by
Lowe & Brydone Printers Limited,
Thetford, Norfolk

Contents

To my mother and father

Foreword

This book brings together four essays on the political thought of Rosa Luxemburg. Some brief remarks on their scope and content are in order here to identify the common set of concerns that has motivated the writing of them. The first essay examines the relationship to Luxemburg's political ideas of her economic theory of capitalist breakdown and disputes the widespread notion that the latter was the basis for a 'spontaneist' conception of the class struggle. In the second essay, her contribution to the debate after 1905 over the nature of the Russian revolution is elaborated, against a common misconception of it, and some of the issues at stake in this debate, including her own views on the nature of bourgeois democracy, are assessed. Building on the point established by the first piece, the third argues that her strategic conception of the mass strike embodied not some irrational faith in mass spontaneity, but the elements of a theory of the political preconditions for successful proletarian revolution, as well as a first adumbration of the difference between bourgeois democracy and socialist democracy. The fourth essay takes up this last question directly, in connection with Luxemburg's criticisms of the Bolsheviks in 1918, and by way of a critique of the kind of interclass and libertarian conceptions which have been used so often to counterpose her to revolutionary Marxism. The first two essays have appeared previously in the *New Left Review,* in the issues for November/December 1973 and January/February 1975 respectively; the last two were written since then.

Apart from the substantive links connecting the topics of these essays, they are unified by three further considerations. In each case – on capitalist breakdown, on the nature of the coming revolution in Russia, on the mass strike, on socialist democracy – one is dealing with a question where Luxemburg has been badly misunderstood and where the effort of simple *recovery* is far from complete. Secondly, each of these questions has a historical significance extending beyond the boundaries of her own specific meaning, because in fact each of them formed the centre of a major politico-theoretical controversy in the history of the international workers' movement. They are matters of interest to anyone interested in this history. Thirdly, they are matters that have not lost their currency but that have, on the contrary, continued to be important. The diagnosis of the tendencies of capitalist development and the articulation to it of a strategy for socialism; the nature of revolutions outside the advanced capitalist countries and the relationship of democratic to socialist tasks; the place of extra-parliamentary, mass struggle in the battle for socialism; the nature of socialist democracy – these are all questions that remain, in one sense or another, open. They continue to be debated amongst socialists today and a great deal hinges on the answers to them. In that sense, to speak of Rosa Luxemburg's political *legacy* is not to consign her to a vanished past, as more than one non-Marxist writer has wanted to. It is to emphasise the actuality of her thought, and to try to appropriate to the present the most valuable elements of it. One does not have to think that her work is beyond criticism, nor is that the spirit of these essays, in order to believe that there are things in it of lasting value.

It is such a belief, and certain inadequacies in the existing literature about her, which together constitute the *raison d'être* of this book. More perhaps than other great revolutionaries, in any case at least as much, Luxemburg has suffered from the usual combination of misunderstanding with outright distortion. In her own case, it succeeded in burying her real political positions in relative obscurity for several decades after her death. Recently, this situation has begun to change for the better and there is today a growing body of serious literature about her. For the English reader in particular, access to her thought has been made immeasurably easier in the last ten years by the appearance of three different though overlapping collections of her political writings, by the publication of one new biography and the republication of an older one long out of print, by the first translation into English of several items of importance from Luxemburg's own 'Anti-Critique' to Lukacs' *History and Class Consciousness*. Nevertheless, in this matter as in others, the weight of the past is not easily shifted, and her work remains even now the subject of wild assertion and arbitrary or mistaken imputation. In the approach to her ideas there is often, even amongst serious students of them, a lack of analytical care and an insufficiently rigorous regard for the detail of her formulations. All of this helps to explain why there should be in both the structure and the style of the following essays the similarity that each presents and assesses some aspect of Luxemburg's political thought through a *critique* of misconceptions which are documented by reference to the existing literature. That similarity reflects something of the posthumous fate of her work. It goes without saying that this book is also indebted to the same body of literature, and every effort has been made to record that debt as well. It is also needless to say, given the very form of the book, that it makes no pretence to being an exhaustive treatment of her life or ideas. It is intended only as a contribution to clarifying them.

I should like to thank Michael Lowy, Robin Blackburn and Perry Anderson, who at various times discussed various points with me as well as giving me encouragement. More especially, I should like to express my gratitude to Adèle Geras who, stage by stage, and more or less line by line, went through the writing of this book with me. Responsibility for its contents remains, of course, my own.

Manchester, December 1975

Barbarism and the Collapse of Capitalism[1]

'Capitalism, by mightily furthering the development of the productive forces, and in virtue of its inherent contradictions, . . . provide(s) an excellent soil for the historical progress of society towards new economic and social forms.' Rosa Luxemburg[2]

'No medicinal herbs can grow in the dirt of capitalist society which can help cure capitalist anarchy.' Rosa Luxemburg[3]

'In her work we see how the last flowering of capitalism is transformed into a ghastly dance of death.' Georg Lukacs[4]

Amongst the misconceptions by which Rosa Luxemburg's thought has been deformed, the most widespread and tenacious is, without doubt, that which attributes to her a thesis going variously under the names of determinism, fatalism and spontaneism. Any one of a number of her real or alleged views can be cited as the manifestation or consequence of this thesis: her emphasis on mass spontaneity; her under-estimation of the importance of organisation and of leadership;

---

[1] Many of the references in this book are to three recent English collections of Luxemburg's political writings, namely: M.-A. Waters (ed.), *Rosa Luxemburg Speaks*, New York, 1970; D. Howard (ed.), *Selected Political Writings of Rosa Luxemburg*, New York and London, 1971; R. Looker (ed.), *Rosa Luxemburg: Selected Political Writings*, London, 1972. These are referred to herein as Waters, Howard and Looker respectively.

[2] R. Luxemburg, *The Accumulation of Capital*, London, 1963, p. 271.

[3] 'Speech to the Stuttgart Congress (1898)', Howard, p. 42.

[4] G. Lukacs, *History and Class Consciousness*, London, 1971, pp. 32–3.

her belief that class consciousness is the simple and direct product of the class struggle of the masses. But what is generally regarded as its ultimate source and cited as definitive proof of its existence is her theory of capitalist breakdown, according to which the contradictions of capitalism must lead, eventually, but also automatically and inevitably, to its complete collapse. Now, there are problems about the very meaning of this notion of final collapse and these will be taken up later on. For the moment it suffices to record that its attribution to Luxemburg is perfectly well founded, for the notion is integral to her thought.

Thus, it is one of the major and recurring themes of her interventions in the great revisionist controversy at the turn of the century. During the 'Bernstein debate' which took place at the Hanover Congress of the SPD in 1899, she argued that it was precisely 'the concept of a breakdown, of a social catastrophe . . . a cataclysm' that distinguished Marxism from reformist gradualism.[5] The same point was emphasised in her most important work of the period, *Social Reform or Revolution,* in which the theory of capitalist collapse was said to be 'the cornerstone of scientific socialism' and its meaning spelled out in the following terms: 'Capitalism, as a result of its own inner contradictions, moves toward a point when it will be unbalanced, when it will simply become impossible . . . the growing anarchy of capitalist economy lead(s) inevitably to its ruin.'[6] All this was, of course, directed against the revisionist argument that capitalism had found, in such institutions as cartels, credit and democracy, the mechanisms of adaptation which, by mitigating capitalist contradictions, made revolution impossible and unnecessary. However, Luxemburg's emphasis on inevitable capitalist breakdown cannot, on this account, be explained away as the result of polemical exaggeration on her part. A decade and a half later, in 1913, she published *The Accumulation of Capital,* her major contribution to Marxist political economy, and in it

[5] 'Speech to the Hanover Congress (1899)', Howard, pp. 48–9.
[6] 'Social Reform or Revolution', Waters, pp. 83, 39.

she tried to provide a rigorous theoretical foundation for the breakdown argument.

The central contention of that work, briefly stated, is that in a closed capitalist economy, consisting of only capitalists and workers and without contact with non-capitalist social formations, the realisation and capitalisation of surplus-value, and hence the accumulation of capital, are impossible. The accumulation process demands access to the markets and the products of a non-capitalist environment, but the very same process progressively deprives itself of that environment by eroding all non-capitalist strata and forms and bringing them under the sway of purely capitalist relations. As Luxemburg puts it, 'capitalism needs non-capitalist social organisations as the setting for its development, (but) it proceeds by assimilating the very conditions which alone can ensure its own existence'.[7] The identification of this contradiction serves the double purpose of explaining the contemporary phenomena of imperialism which is a 'competitive struggle for what remains still open of the non-capitalist environment',[8] and of specifying the *economic* limit or term of capitalist society. The relentless logic of her position is that the accumulation of capital, and the attempt, by imperialism, to secure for it the non-capitalist consumers and products which make it possible, must lead eventually to a situation of 'exclusive and universal domination of capitalist production in all countries and for all branches of industry'. Once this happens, there is no non-capitalist environment left: 'Accumulation must come to a stop. The realisation and capitalisation of surplus value become impossible to accomplish . . . the collapse of capitalism follows inevitably, as an objective historical necessity.'[9] Now, it is true that even in *The Accumulation of Capital*, where Luxemburg says almost nothing about the concrete forms of proletarian class struggle, this catastrophist vision is tempered by the qualification that the limit of capitalist accumulation is a theoretical one, which will never actually be reached; the

[7] *The Accumulation of Capital,* p. 366.
[8] *ibid.,* p. 446.
[9] *ibid.,* p. 417.

revolt of the international working class against the rule of capital will pre-empt it.[10] Despite this qualification, however, it remains the case for her that capitalist society has a purely economic limit in the specific sense that the dynamics of capitalist accumulation must lead to a point where it becomes an impossibility, where, with or without the revolt of the working class, it must inevitably collapse. As we shall see, there is no evidence to suggest that Luxemburg ever abandoned this view.

On the basis of it, and of an impermissible logical leap which simply equates the breakdown of capitalism with the creation of socialism, it is mere child's play to construct a completely fatalist and allegedly Luxemburgist perspective on the revolutionary process. According to this, the laws of capitalist development inevitably issue in economic breakdown and socialist revolution, and the consequence and other face of this catastrophism is spontaneism, contempt for organisation, contempt for leadership, and so on. The same inexorable economic laws which produce capitalist collapse also bring forth mass actions whose spontaneous power and dynamic are sufficient to solve all the political and tactical problems that arise. Taken strictly, this position amounts to the *abolition* of the need for theoretical work, for propaganda and agitation, for organisation and for preparation for the conquest of political power. It amounts to the abolition, in short, of the political and ideological/theoretical dimensions of the struggle for socialism, since the activities (practices) specific to these are taken care of in the end by inexorable economic laws. The perspective, it is clear, is not only fatalist but also economist. That it was purveyed, as a representation of Luxemburg's views, to the whole generation that witnessed the Stalinist destruction of revolutionary Marxism (and not only of that) is a fact which need not detain us for long. As early as 1925 it was quite clearly formulated by Ruth Fischer, whose contribution to the 'Bolshevisation', i.e. Stalinisation, of the Comintern included the attempt to eradicate from the German

[10] *ibid.*, pp. 417, 446, 467.

Communist Party the 'syphilis bacillus' that she took Luxemburg's influence to be: 'Rosa Luxemburg's theory of accumulation . . . is the fount of all errors, all theories of spontaneity, all erroneous conceptions of organisational problems.'[11] What does require close attention, however, is the fact that though this kind of interpretation is the most grotesque caricature of Luxemburg's views, as should be recognised by anyone with even passing familiarity with her work, it continues to lead a subterranean existence. It surfaces here and there with qualifications which are sometimes merely rhetorical and sometimes not, and it does so not only in contemporary socialist literature generally but also in writing devoted specifically to the clarification of Luxemburg's ideas – and even in the best of it. This indicates that the source of the misconception is located in a number of theoretical ambiguities and problems in her own work, and it can only be dispelled if these are resolved. At the same time, the attempt to resolve them is facilitated by a detailed scrutiny of the different forms of this misconception.

As a first approach, then, let us consider a few examples which clearly show the unhappy role which Luxemburg has been cast to play in socialist writing. In a recent critique of Lukacs, Gareth Stedman Jones finds in his early work 'a restatement of the old Luxemburgist and anarcho-syndicalist couplet, economism/spontaneism', though Luxemburg is credited with a 'more sophisticated version' of this than is offered by Lukacs. The grounds for comparison with Luxemburg are Lukacs' belief in the final economic collapse of capitalism that ushers in the socialist revolution and his attribution of the emergence of proletarian consciousness to the advent of full-scale economic crisis.[12] Lucio Magri, in a discussion of the revolutionary party, explains Luxemburg's 'spontaneist vision' by reference to the same kinds of view, though he finds it 'astonishing' that she should have had this

[11] J. P. Nettl, *Rosa Luxemburg,* 2 vols., London, 1966, Vol. 2, pp. 533, 800–1, 805–6.

[12] G. Stedman Jones, 'The Marxism of the Early Lukacs: an Evaluation', *New Left Review,* No. 70, Nov./Dec. 1971, pp. 50–1.

vision since several other of her views contradict it. What is actually astonishing in Magri's case is the argument said by him definitively to separate Lenin from spontaneism: 'The passage from capitalism to socialism was never for him an inevitable process, a fatality dictated by the objective forces of development within capitalist society. On the contrary, he argued that . . . in their spontaneous development they would merely lead to a crisis of civilisation, a new Dark Age.'[13] This argument is Rosa Luxemburg's. Ernest Mandel, discussing the Leninist theory of organisation, and basing himself not on the theory of capitalist collapse but on a single sentence from her polemic against Lenin in 1904, attributes to Luxemburg a conception according to which experience in struggle, in mass actions, is sufficient for the achievement of an adequate class consciousness and of the proletariat's historical objectives; a conception which is counterposed by her to the need for consistent preparation and education of workers and for the formation and schooling of a proletarian vanguard. For her, according to Mandel, the revolutionary party 'will be created by the revolutionary action of the masses'. He also says, however, that 'the so-called theory of spontaneity . . . can be attributed to Luxemburg only with important reservations'.[14] The reservations do indeed turn out to be important: in a subsequent text devoted to analysing the unity and importance of Luxemburg's activity and work – and which, it should be said, is an excellent contribution to that project of *recovery* – Mandel affirms that she was never guilty of the very conceptions ('enfantillages') attributed to her in his text on organisation.[15]

It should be evident from all this that there is a problem about simply attaching the spontaneist label to Luxemburg, and hence the qualifications and contradictions which arise whenever she is used, negatively and polemically, as the con-

[13] L. Magri, 'Problems of the Marxist Theory of the Revolutionary Party', *New Left Review,* No. 60, March/April 1970, pp. 107–8, 105.

[14] E. Mandel, *The Leninist Theory of Organisation,* London, 1971, pp. 6–7, 24, 8.

[15] E. Mandel, 'Rosa et la social-démocratie allemande', *Quatrième Internationale,* No. 48, March 1971, p. 18.

venient bearer of it. This use of her is problematic because, on reading her work, one is confronted at every turn with concepts and arguments which radically separate her Marxism from that determinist science of iron economic laws which is the usual foundation of fatalism and spontaneism. In order to begin to establish this, it is necessary to quote at length from writings scattered over a period of two decades, confining the exercise for the moment to statements of a very general kind. That they are not mere empty or rhetorical gestures on Luxemburg's part, but founded, on the contrary, on concrete political and tactical conceptions which reduce the spontaneist/fatalist charge to nought, is a contention which we will endeavour to prove in due course.

In *Social Reform or Revolution* which, as we have seen, insists on the inevitability of capitalist collapse, Luxemburg also argues that 'the present procedure of the Social Democracy does not consist in waiting for the antagonisms of capitalism to develop and in passing on, only then, to the task of suppressing them. On the contrary, the essence of revolutionary procedure is to be guided by the direction of this development, once it is ascertained, and inferring from this direction what consequences are necessary for the political struggle.'[16] The thought which is expressed ambiguously in this passage is reiterated, this time clearly, in a text on militarism which dates from the same period: 'In relation to the military system Schippel doesn't understand, just as Bernstein doesn't understand in relation to capitalism as a whole, that society's objective development merely gives us *the preconditions* of a higher level of development, but that without our *conscious interference*, without the *political struggle* of the working class for a socialist transformation or for a militia, *neither the one nor the other will ever come about.*'[17] What these passages say, to anticipate somewhat, is that if the collapse of capitalism is 'written', as a blind fatality, in its objective economic antagonisms, the creation of socialism is

[16] 'Social Reform or Revolution', Waters, p. 60.
[17] 'Militia and Militarism', Howard, p. 144; last emphasis added.

not. The latter requires a conscious political struggle on the part of the working class.

Nor is this a working class without organisation and leadership whose elemental power alone permits it to storm Heaven. Luxemburg's mass strike pamphlet of 1906, which is often regarded as the seat of such a metaphysic, explicitly repudiates it: 'The Social-Democrats are the most enlightened, most class-conscious vanguard of the proletariat. They cannot and dare not wait, in a fatalist fashion, with folded arms for the advent of the "revolutionary situation" . . . they must now, as always, hasten the development of things and endeavour to accelerate events.' Though it is not in the party's power actually to create a revolutionary situation, 'what it can and must do is to make clear the political tendencies, when they once appear, and to formulate them as resolute and consistent tactics'.[18] Putting this in a nutshell, Luxemburg wrote in 1915: 'Passive fatalism can never be the role of a revolutionary party like the Social Democracy.'[19]

Two more passages will suffice to complete the general point being made here. They also date from 1915. The first, which measures Social Democracy's capitulation to the First World War against what it supposedly stood for in the preceding decades, may be regarded as Luxemburg's own 'thesis on Feuerbach': 'Just as in Marx himself the roles of acute historical analyst and bold revolutionary, the man of ideas and the man of action were inseparably bound up, mutually supporting and complementing each other, so for the first time in the history of the modern labour movement the socialist teachings of Marxism united theoretical knowledge with revolutionary energy, the one illuminating and stimulating the other. Both are in equal measure part of the essence of Marxism; each, separated from the other, transforms Marxism into a sad caricature of itself.' Put to the test by an event it had foreseen, Social Democracy proved itself unwilling and

---

[18] 'The Mass Strike, the Political Party and the Trade Unions', Waters, pp. 200, 205.

[19] 'The Junius Pamphlet', Waters, p. 311.

unable, on the basis of that understanding, actually to *make* history.[20]

The second passage is the much quoted one from *The Junius Pamphlet*. It is quoted here again at such length because the argument being pursued turns upon it:

'Man does not make history of his own volition, but he makes history nevertheless. The proletariat is dependent in its actions upon the degree of [maturity] to which social evolution has advanced. But again, social evolution is not a thing apart from the proletariat; it is in the same measure its driving force and its cause as well as its product and its effect. And though we can no more skip a period in our historical development than a man can jump over his shadow, it lies within our power to accelerate or to retard it. . . . The final victory of the socialist proletariat . . . will never be accomplished, if the burning spark of the conscious will of the masses does not spring from the material conditions that have been built up by past development. Socialism will not fall as manna from heaven. It can only be won by a long chain of powerful struggles, in which the proletariat, under the leadership of the Social Democracy, will learn to take hold of the rudder of society to become instead of the powerless victim of history, its conscious guide. Friedrich Engels once said: "Capitalist society faces a dilemma, either an advance to socialism or a reversion to barbarism".[21] . . . We stand today, as Friedrich Engels prophesied more than a generation ago, before the awful proposition: either the triumph of imperialism and the destruction of all culture, and, as in ancient Rome, depopulation, desolation, degeneration, a vast cemetry; or, the victory of socialism, that is, the conscious struggle of the international proletariat against imperialism, against its methods, against war. This is the dilemma of world history, its inevitable choice,

[20] 'Rebuilding the International', Looker, p. 209. A similar passage, dating from 1907, is cited in L. Basso, 'Rosa Luxemburg: the Dialectical Method', *International Socialist Journal,* No. 16–17, Nov. 1966, pp. 525–6.

[21] The reference is probably to F. Engels, *Anti-Dühring,* Moscow, 1959, pp. 217–8; cf. also pp. 228, 386.

whose scales are trembling in the balance awaiting the decision of the proletariat. Upon it depends the future of culture and humanity.'[22]

Socialism *or* barbarism! This affirmation of a historical alternative, of an outcome still to be decided and in genuine doubt, is no mere passing thought on Luxemburg's part. She repeated it many times and in the last months of her life, during the German revolution, she wrote it into the proclamations, and into the very programme, of the Spartacus League.[23]

Yet, the simple rehearsal of all this far from settles everything, as some of the interpretative literature on Luxemburg suggests that it might. For example, Cliff, who makes reference to it in order to justify the assertion that Luxemburg's 'non-fatalistic' perspective did not presuppose the inevitability of socialism, shows no awareness that certain aspects of her work might render the demonstration, rather than assertion, of this point problematic.[24] Others are more sensitive to the existence of such a problem, but only in the sense that they transfer it from her work into their own, reproduce it rather than solve it. Thus, Frölich's book emphatically acquits her of fatalism, objectivism and spontaneism,[25] but refers at the same time to her conviction of the inevitability and historical necessity of socialism, this being the only possible issue of certain capitalist collapse.[26] A passing allusion to 'the dialectical character of historical necessity' is hardly a satisfactory resolution, more especially since the meaning Frölich gives this is that human activity affects only the 'more or less rapid' fulfilment of what are in any case 'iron laws of historical development'.[27] Similarly, Howard argues that for Luxemburg socialism is a necessity, the result of 'an internally self-contradictory system which *must* eventually break down and

[22] 'The Junius Pamphlet', Waters, p. 269.

[23] See 'To the Proletariat of All Lands' and 'What Does the Spartakusbund Want?', Looker, pp. 269, 275–7.

[24] T. Cliff, *Rosa Luxemburg,* London, 1968, pp. 94, 37–8.

[25] P. Frölich, *Rosa Luxemburg,* London, 1972, pp. 49–51, 140–4, 163.

[26] *ibid.*, pp. 49, 159.

[27] *ibid.*, p. 144. But see n. 47 of this essay on a different resolution.

lead to a revolutionary transformation';[28] but it is not a 'metaphysical' or 'mechanical' necessity, and her view is contrasted with that dominant in the SPD, 'a non-dialectical, determinist view of the world which argued that socialism was objectively necessary'.[29]

The intention here is not to make cheap debating points at the expense of writers the value of whose work in rescuing Luxemburg's ideas from distortion and misunderstanding is beyond question. It is simply to point to an unsettled difficulty in their work and terminology, one which reflects an identical difficulty in hers. *Prima facie* at least there may appear to be a contradiction between her political economy, which predicates automatic capitalist collapse on a simple economic mechanism, namely, the eventual impossibility of accumulation, and the resolute refusal, embodied in her political activity and *theory*, to countenance any form of economism or to wait for that economic process to work itself out. This contradiction, it will be shown, is more apparent than real. But if some have taken it for real, concluding either that the refusal is only a gesture which masks a basically economistic conception, or that between her political economy and her political theory there is a gulf which cannot be bridged, there are certain ambiguous formulations in Luxemburg's work which explain why they might have done so. In these she gives expression to her revolutionary optimism, to her confidence in the victory of socialism, by speaking of the creation of socialism and the collapse of capitalism in the same terms, assimilating the one to the other as if they were the same thing, determined by the same economic laws and both equally inevitable or necessary. If there is anything which can be said to mask the meaning of Luxemburg's work, it is formulations such as these. In any case, it would be tendentious to ignore their existence, and so a few examples, drawn again from writings which cover a period of twenty years, will be cited.

In her contribution to the debate over revisionism, in propounding her theory of accumulation, and in defending

[28] Howard, pp. 12, 14; emphasis added.
[29] *ibid.*, pp. 15 n. 9, 16, 33.

that theory against its critics, Luxemburg insisted that socialism was a 'historical necessity'.[30] She argued: in 1899, that the 'inevitability' of proletarian victory was demonstrated by scientific socialism; in 1915, that the same thing was 'assured' by the 'inexorable laws of history'; and at the end of 1918, that it was 'guaranteed' by the 'prepotent law of historical determinism'.[31] Finally, the elision or reduction on which such statements were based is evident when she speaks, in 1899, of 'the inevitability of [capitalist] collapse, leading – *and this is only another aspect of the same phenomenon* – to socialism';[32] or when she asserts, in 1915, that 'the rebellion of the workers, the class struggle, is only the ideological reflection of the objective historical necessity of socialism, resulting from the objective impossibility of capitalism at a certain economic stage';[33] or when she argues, in 1918, that 'it is the objective insolubility of the tasks confronting bourgeois society that makes socialism a historical necessity and the world revolution inevitable'.[34] That these formulations mask rather than present Luxemburg's meaning we will now proceed to show by examining and rebutting two attempts to cope with the contradiction to which they give rise.

The first attempt is that of the late Peter Nettl, and is succinctly resumed in the following judgement: 'Rosa Luxemburg always postulated failure as an alternative to the successful resolution of the dialectic; chaos or defeat could engulf the emerging society. There was nothing inevitable or automatic about her doctrine – provided one does not rely on *The Accumulation of Capital* alone.'[35] In other words, for Nettl, there is indeed a contradiction in Luxemburg's work

[30] 'Social Reform or Revolution', Waters, p. 63; *The Accumulation of Capital,* p. 325; 'The Accumulation of Capital – an Anti-Critique', in R. Luxemburg and N. Bukharin, *Imperialism and the Accumulation of Capital,* London, 1972, p. 77. This last text is referred to henceforth as 'Anti-Critique'.

[31] 'Social Reform or Revolution', 'The Junius Pamphlet' and 'Speech to the Founding Convention of the German Communist Party', Waters, pp. 86, 264, 415.

[32] 'Social Reform or Revolution', Waters, p. 68; emphasis added.

[33] 'Anti-Critique', p. 76.

[34] 'Fragment sur la guerre, la question nationale et la révolution' in R. Luxemburg, *Oeuvres II : Ecrits politiques 1917–1918,* Paris, 1969, p. 99.

[35] Nettl, *op. cit.,* Vol. 2, p. 538.

between the affirmation and denial of determinism, the theory of accumulation and collapse being identified as the site of the first, while the socialism-or-barbarism formula is regarded as at least one indication of the second. In order to make some sense of this contradiction, he simply drives a wedge between *The Accumulation of Capital* and the rest of Luxemburg's writings and activities. The former was the product of purely theoretical preoccupations concerning Marx's reproduction schemes in Volume II of *Capital*,[36] and the economic explanation of imperialism which it 'incidentally' provided had 'no obvious connection' with her political writings on the same subject. These two aspects of her work were 'kept in separate compartments' and there is no evidence to suggest that she ever tried to relate the theoretical economic analysis to her concrete political concerns. Had she done so, this would indeed have meant 'a propensity to spontaneity and objective automatism, only mitigated by the specific recommendations to action'. And the most likely explanation as to why she did not do so is a tactical one: she wished to avoid justifying the kind of theory of spontaneity and political inaction of which she was later accused.[37] In short, the contradiction exists in Luxemburg's work, but one of its terms is consigned to *The Accumulation of Capital* and that work itself is tucked away in the closet of her exclusively theoretical concerns. On the part of an author who devoted long and arduous labour to the most detailed study of Luxemburg's life and work, this judgement constitutes a failure of perception bordering on the fantastic. Each of its arguments is demonstrably false.

In the first place, there *is* an obvious connection between the economic explanation of imperialism and her political writings on the same subject, sufficiently obvious at any rate to have been noticed by a fair number of her readers.[38] The economic analysis claimed to lay bare the roots of those

---

[36] Not Volume III as is incorrectly stated at p. 530.

[37] *ibid.*, pp. 530–6. Cf. Waters (p. 19) who seems to follow this line of argument.

[38] See, for example, I. Fetscher's 'Postcript' to Frölich, *op. cit.*, p. 308; E. H. Carr, *1917 : Before and After,* London, 1969, pp. 47–9; E. Mandel, 'Rosa et la social-démocratie allemande', *loc. cit.*, p. 19; Looker, p. 29.

phenomena, such as colonialism, militarism, tariffs, the collapse of bourgeois liberalism, etc., to which Luxemburg's political writings of the period repeatedly and urgently drew attention in an effort to alert the SPD against the danger they represented and to mobilise it against them.[39] Secondly, there *is* evidence that Luxemburg, aware of the connection, related the theoretical analysis of accumulation to her concrete political concerns. The *Anti-Critique,* written in prison in 1915 in defence of that analysis, begins with a brief recapitulation of it and then continues in the following unambiguous terms:

'At first glance it may appear to be a purely theoretical exercise. And yet the practical meaning of the problem is at hand – the connection with the most outstanding fact of our time: imperialism. The typical external phenomena of imperialism: competition among capitalist countries to win colonies and spheres of interest, opportunities for investment, the international loan system, militarism, tariff barriers, the dominant role of finance capital and trusts in world politics, are all well known. Its connection with the final phase of capitalism, its importance for accumulation, are so blatantly open that it is clearly acknowledged by its supporters as well as its enemies. But Social Democracy refuses to be satisfied with this empirical knowledge. It must search for the precise economic rules behind appearances, to find the actual roots of this large and colourful complex of imperialist phenomena. As always in these cases, only precise theoretical knowledge of the problem at its roots can provide our practical struggle against imperialism with security, aim and force – essential for the politics of the proletariat.'[40]

Thirdly, Luxemburg felt perfectly able to make the connection for which Nettl claims there is no evidence, because,

[39] See, for example, 'Peace Utopias', Waters, pp. 250–4; 'Concerning Morocco' and 'What Now?', Looker, pp. 166, 172–3, 175–6; 'The Idea of May Day on the March', Howard, pp. 317–20.

[40] 'Anti-Critique', p. 60.

so far from fearing that to do so would be to justify a policy of inaction, she saw her theory of accumulation and collapse in the opposite light. It gave firm foundation to a stance of *revolutionary* opposition to imperialism and rendered utopian the hopes of the SPD 'centre' that disarmament, a peaceful federation of democratic states, a more moderate imperialism, might be achieved by alliance with the bourgeoisie. In this view she was confirmed by the hostile reception accorded to *The Accumulation of Capital* by the theoretical representatives of that political tendency.[41] Fourthly and crucially: independent of Luxemburg's own judgement on it, in which she may after all have been wrong, the theoretical analysis of that book provides no basis for spontaneism and 'objective automatism'. This last point can be demonstrated by considering the precise significance of the socialism-or-barbarism formula.

We now summarise the argument of the one text to have focused on the importance of this formula, and to have done so with a degree of analytical rigour which is rare in the literature dealing with Luxemburg's relation to spontaneism and economism. Michael Lowy has argued recently[42] that the same optimistic and passive fatalism which was the central axis of Kautsky's vision of the world and dominant in the SPD's theory and practice, represented a 'temptation' in Luxemburg's thought prior to the outbreak of the First World War. In her opposition to Bernstein's attempt to base the struggle for socialism not on the objective contradictions of capitalism but on timeless moral principles like justice (his invocation of Kant against cant),[43] she gave expression to this temptation in a number of arguments. Lowy refers to those in *Social Reform or Revolution* according to which the anarchy of capitalist economy leads inevitably to its ruin, its insoluble contradictions to inevitable collapse, and in which the class

---

[41] *ibid.*, p. 148. Cf. P. M. Sweezy, *The Theory of Capitalist Development,* London, 1946, pp. 206–7; and *The Present As History,* New York, 1953, p. 294.

[42] M. Lowy, 'Il significato metodologico della parola d'ordine "socialismo o barbarie"', *Problemi del Socialismo,* 3° serie, anno XIII, no. 1, 1971. Reprinted, in French, in M. Lowy, *Dialectique et Révolution,* Paris 1973, pp. 113–25.

[43] E. Bernstein, *Evolutionary Socialism,* New York, 1961, pp. 200–24.

consciousness of the proletariat is said to be the simple intellectual reflection of these contradictions and of this imminent
breakdown.[44] Even Luxemburg's refusal to countenance the
purely passive tactic of waiting does not escape from a fatalist
frame of reference since it is formulated in terms of accelerating a process which is in any case unilinear and inevitable,
and in which therefore the conscious political intervention of
a revolutionary party can only be an auxiliary, and not strictly
necessary, element.[45] That all this was only a temptation in
Luxemburg's thought in this period can be seen from her
dissatisfaction, after 1905, with the purely parliamentary
tactic, from her polemic, after 1910, against the endorsement
of it in Kautsky's so-called strategy of 'attrition', and from
her long struggle within the SPD for the adoption of the mass
strike orientation. But though these positions helped to put
some distance between her and any full-blown fatalist problematic, it was only when the catastrophe of 4 August 1914
destroyed her conviction in the irresistible necessity of the
advent of socialism that she broke definitively with it.

And that break, Lowy argues, was expressed in *The Junius
Pamphlet,* in the slogan 'socialism or barbarism'. Its importance, according to him, hinges not on the content or meaning
of the term 'barbarism' but on the very principle of a historical
alternative: 'What is important, theoretically *decisive* in the
formula is not "barbarism" but "*socialism or . . .*".'[46] That
is to say, there is not one direction of development, there are
several, and the role of the proletariat under the leadership of
its party is not simply to accelerate the historical process but
to decide it. Socialism is not the inevitable product of iron
economic laws but an 'objective possibility' defined by the
socio-economic conditions of capitalism. In the actualisation
of that possibility, the subjective factor, the conscious political
intervention of the proletariat, is the decisive, and not an
auxiliary, element. Thus, it is only in 1915, according to

[44] 'Social Reform or Revolution', Waters, pp. 39–41. Cf. above n. 6 and text.

[45] 'Social Reform or Revolution', Waters, p. 60, and a passage cited in Frölich,
op. cit., p. 143. Cf. above n. 16 and text.

[46] Lowy, *loc. cit.*

Lowy, that Luxemburg's thought becomes truly coherent and escapes from the logic of political passivity implicit in the belief in the inevitability of socialism.[47]

Lowy's argument, in both its merits and its mistakes, conducts us to the threshold of a solution to the problem under discussion. By its clear and rigorous definition of the problem, it correctly identifies the significance of the socialism-or-barbarism formula: the possibility which it offers of giving coherent foundation to a non-fatalist, non-economistic and revolutionary Marxism. At the same time, while to the best of our knowledge that formula makes its first appearance in Luxemburg's writings in *The Junius Pamphlet* in 1915, there are grounds for scepticism concerning the periodisation of her work which Lowy uses that fact to support. First: not a single one of the formulations and arguments cited by him as evidence of a fatalist temptation in Luxemburg's thought before 1915 disappears from her writings after that date. Reference has already been made to the category of assertion which, before and *after* 1915, predicates the necessity of socialism on inexorable laws and reduces the proletarian class struggle to an epiphenomenon of economic contradictions and of incipient capitalist collapse; indeed one such reference was to *The Junius Pamphlet* itself.[48] Again, in the very passage from that work on which Lowy's argument turns, the socialism-or-barbarism formula sits happily beside the argument that it is in the proletariat's power 'to accelerate or to retard' historical development.[49] Further, the theory of inevitable capitalist collapse, as has already been said, is not confined to Luxemburg's interventions in the revisionist controversy. On the contrary, it received extensive theoretical elaboration in *The Accumulation of Capital* in 1913, was vigorously defended against criticism in the *Anti-Critique* in 1915, and was reaffirmed in the *Introduction to Political Economy* which she began to prepare for publication in prison

---

[47] In the preface to the second German edition of his book, Frölich (*op. cit.*, pp. xvi–xvii) suggests a similar periodisation.

[48] See above notes 30–4 and text.

[49] See above n. 22 and text.

in 1916 (but which was never in fact published in her life-time).[50]

Secondly and conversely: in Luxemburg's writings before the First World War there is no shortage of formulations which play the same role as the slogan, 'socialism or barbarism', by insisting that the conscious political action of the proletariat is *indispensable* to the creation of socialism. One of these, dating from 1899, has already been mentioned: without the conscious political struggle of the working class the socialist transformation will 'never come about', since the objective development of capitalist society provides its preconditions only.[51] To this may be added the argument of *Social Reform or Revolution* that socialism will be the consequence not only of 'the growing contradictions of capitalist economy', but also of 'the comprehension by the working class of the unavoid-ability of the suppression of these contradictions through a social transformation', also of 'the increased organisation and consciousness of the proletarian class, which constitutes the active factor in the coming revolution'.[52] And to that may be added the following argument of 1903: 'The socialist revolu-tion can only be completed by the working class . . . only the mass struggle, the organisation of the proletariat and its enlightenment can bring about the conditions necessary for the future society.'[53]

The temptation of (propensity to) fatalist economism, if it exists at all, can no more be confined to the pre-War writings than it can to *The Accumulation of Capital*. The break, if *it* exists at all, between that temptation on the one hand and activist revolutionary politics on the other, runs throughout Luxemburg's life and work from beginning to end in the shape of a logical contradiction. The fact of the matter is, however, that neither the one nor the other does exist, and this fact emerges if we pay closer attention, in the socialism-or-barbarism formula, to the *content* of the alternative to socialism

[50] 'What is Economics?', Waters, p. 248.
[51] See above n. 17 and text.
[52] 'Social Reform or Revolution', Waters, pp. 59, 39.
[53] 'In Memory of the Proletariat Party', Howard, p. 196.

it postulates, to the meaning of 'barbarism', rather than just to the formal principle of there being an alternative. For what then becomes apparent is that the idea of inevitable capitalist collapse and the idea of socialism-or-barbarism, the two ideas which Nettl and Lowy, and the literature on Luxemburg more generally, regard as contradictory, opposing them to one another as representatives, respectively, of fatalism and activism – that these two ideas, so far from being contradictory, are not even different. They are *one and the same idea*. For Luxemburg, 'barbarism' signifies nothing other than the collapse of capitalism. Before substantiating this assertion with textual evidence which is conclusive, it is worth spelling out its implications.

The equation of barbarism and capitalist collapse entails that the first like the second is the spontaneous and necessary product of internal economic contradictions, and that it is not socialism but barbarism that is inevitable; a conclusion which may appear paradoxical in a revolutionary Marxist if it is taken to suggest the impossibility of socialism. However, the paradox disappears if we conceive the collapse of capitalism, as Luxemburg undoubtedly did conceive it, as a process of which both the forms and the end result are a species of barbarism. In that event, though the process is indeed unavoidable, it remains an open question whether it will be allowed to run its course down to the last barbaric consequences (and we shall see what this means in a moment), or whether, on the other hand, it will be halted in its early stages by the conscious political intervention of the working class which will prevent the impending catastrophe, by abolishing the contradictions which lead toward it and creating a socialist society. For Luxemburg, therefore, what the inevitability of capitalist collapse proves is not the redundancy, but the urgent indispensability, of conscious revolutionary struggle on the part of the working class. It is because of that inevitability, and not despite it, that such a struggle is required. It is also because of that inevitability that Luxemburg can meaningfully speak of there being an alternative to socialism. For what else, other than catastrophe, could that alternative be? The indefinite existence of capitalism? Some new form of class domination? Not a line in her work so much as hints at a belief in such possibilities. The whole breakdown theory gives sense to the slogan 'socialism or barbarism', distinguishing it from mere rhetoric; it is its meaning and not, as has so often been supposed, its negation.

Apart from the connotations of cruelty it carries, barbarism, as any dictionary will tell you, is a condition of being uncivilised and uncultured. If we take that literally, and eschew the usage according to which civilisations and cultures which are simply other and alien are labelled barbarian, then barbarism can only mean the complete absence of culture and civilisation . . . total social breakdown, chaos. That is Luxemburg's meaning. As Nettl himself has perceptively noted, 'The continuity of chaos as a looming alternative to dialectical progress . . . strangely resembles the chronological continuity of the state of nature menacing "failed" societies in Hobbes's *Leviathan.*'[54] But that same chaotic condition is also the end point of the catastrophic collapse of capitalism if the proletarian revolution does not intercede to prevent its being reached. At the same time, even before it is reached, the forms taken by the process of collapse are sufficiently disruptive and destructive to count, for Luxemburg, as incipient forms of barbarism. That none of this is an arbitrary imputation to Luxemburg can now be shown by citing the relevant texts from her work. We will quote, first, some passages from her political writings which deal ostensibly with barbarism, then, some passages from her economic writings which deal with the collapse of capitalism. The solidarity between them is evident and leaves no room for doubt.

1. 'What does a "reversion to barbarism" mean at the present stage of European civilisation? . . . *This world war* means a reversion to barbarism. The triumph of imperialism leads to the destruction of culture, sporadically during a modern war, and forever, if the period of world wars that has just

[54] Nettl, *op. cit.*, Vol. 2, p. 538 n. 1.

begun is allowed to take its damnable course to the last ultimate consequence . . . the destruction of all culture . . . depopulation, desolation, degeneration, a vast cemetery.'

'Shamed, dishonoured, wading in blood and dripping with filth, thus capitalist society stands. Not as we usually see it, playing the roles of peace and righteousness, of order, of philosophy, of ethics – as a roaring beast, as an orgy of anarchy, as a pestilential breath, devastating culture and humanity – so it appears in all its hideous nakedness.'[55]

'The imperialist phase of the rule of capitalism has indeed made peace illusory by actually declaring the dictatorship of militarism – war – to be permanent.'

'Either world war to the verge of universal ruin or proletarian revolution – imperialism or socialism.'

'Humanity is faced with this alternative: dissolution and decline into capitalist anarchy or rebirth through social revolution.'

'The world war has faced society with this alternative: either continuation of capitalism, new wars and an early decline into chaos and anarchy, or the abolition of capitalist exploitation.'[56]

'Our solution offers the only means of saving human society from destruction. . . . Today mankind is faced with two alternatives: It may perish amid chaos; or it may find salvation in socialism.'[57]

2. 'The more violently, ruthlessly and thoroughly imperialism brings about the decline of non-capitalist civilisations, the more rapidly it cuts the very ground from under the feet of capitalist accumulation. Though imperialism is the historical method for prolonging the career of capitalism, it is also a sure means of bringing it to a swift conclusion. This is not to say that capitalist development must be actually driven to this extreme: the mere tendency towards imperialism

[55] 'The Junius Pamphlet', Waters, pp. 269, 262; cf. also pp. 325–8.

[56] 'Rebuilding the International', 'The Old Mole', 'To the Proletariat of All Lands' and 'What Does the Spartakusbund Want?', Looker, pp. 204, 234, 269, 275.

[57] 'Speech to the Founding Convention of the German Communist Party', Waters, p. 412.

of itself takes forms which make the final phase of capitalism a period of catastrophe.'

'Capitalism prepares its own downfall under ever more violent contortions and convulsions.'

'The more ruthlessly capital sets about the destruction of non-capitalist strata at home and in the outside world . . . the greater also is the change in the day-to-day history of capital. It becomes a string of political and social disasters and convulsions, and under these conditions, punctuated by periodical economic catastrophes or crises, accumulation can go on no longer.'[58]

'Expansion has accompanied the entire history of capitalism and in its present, final, imperialist phase, it has adopted such an unbridled character that it puts the whole civilisation of mankind in question.'

'Imperialism brings catastrophe as a mode of existence back from the periphery of capitalist development to its point of departure. The expansion of capital, which for four centuries had given the existence and civilisation of all non-capitalist peoples in Asia, Africa, America and Australia over to ceaseless convulsions and general and complete decline, is now plunging the civilised peoples of Europe itself into a series of catastrophes whose final result can only be the decline of civilisation or the transition to the socialist mode of production. Seen in this light, the position of the proletariat with regard to imperialism leads to a general confrontation with the rule of capital. The specific rules of its conduct are given by that historical alternative.'[59]

'Marx . . . discovered how these same laws regulating the present economy work towards its collapse, by the increasing anarchy which more and more endangers the very existence of society itself, by assembling a chain of devastating economic and political catastrophes. . . . The inherent tendencies of capitalist development, at a certain point of their maturity, necessitate the transition to a planful mode of production consciously organised by the entire working force of society –

[58] *The Accumulation of Capital*, pp. 446, 453, 466–7.
[59] 'Anti-Critique', pp. 143, 147–8.

in order that all of society and human civilisation might not perish in the convulsions of uncontrolled anarchy. . . . Socialism becomes a *historic necessity,* because it is a result of the operation of the very laws of capitalist development.'[60]

When Luxemburg was condemned by Otto Bauer for offering a conception of capitalist collapse which placed the whole emphasis on 'the mechanical impossibility of realising surplus value' and none on the action of the 'educated, united and organised' working class, she contemptuously repudiated the charge.[61] In the light of the preceding argument and the above documentation, one can see that both the charge and its repudiation are well founded. Bauer was referring to the thesis, which is unquestionably there, that the approaching impossibility of accumulation, in itself and quite regardless of the dispositions of the working class, spelled doom for capitalist society. Luxemburg, for her part, was referring to the contention that the catastrophic nature of this process was such as to make the revolutionary conquest of power by the proletariat a task of utmost urgency. And this, in terms of the argument here being made, is the essential point. For, if it is true that she subscribed to a theory of capitalist breakdown based ultimately on the postulation of purely economic disequilibria, and in *that* sense economist, it is also true that this did not serve as the springboard toward what is more usually understood by 'economism': the denigration or underestimation of theory and ideological combat, of political organisation and leadership, uncritical faith in the power of 'spontaneity', etc. It did not because it could not, the collapse of capitalism and the creation of socialism not being identified in Luxemburg's mind. 'Left to itself', capitalism in collapse could no more become an authentic socialist society than can a patch of ground, barren through neglect, become a field of wheat. Capitalism could not become socialism by the dynamic of its economic laws alone. What it offered was some preconditions and a threat and it required a concerted initiative

[60] 'What is Economics?', Waters, p. 248.
[61] 'Anti-Critique', p. 149.

on the part of the proletarian historical agent to put the first to good use and to pre-empt the second.

If this is so, how can one account for the fact that Luxemburg did sometimes speak of revolutionary political initiatives as the mere accelerators of a unilinear process, of socialist revolution as simply the other face of capitalist collapse, of socialism as a historical necessity or inevitability? That such formulations are ambiguous is a point which has already been conceded and there can be no question of trying to explain them all away. Nevertheless, at the risk of special pleading, some considerations may be offered in extenuation. First, this kind of terminology was the common language of all Marxists of the period, from Kautsky through to Lenin,[62] a usage which in no way abolished the real differences between them with regard to revolutionary politics. Secondly, these statements may have a psychological meaning. They may reflect Luxemburg's confidence in the ability of the proletariat to wage its class struggle to a successful conclusion, her revolutionary optimism that, in view of the alternative, they would surely do so, her faith in the victory of socialism. But such *psychological* qualities, essential to some degree in every revolutionary, are by themselves not equivalent to the *theoretical* conception according to which socialist revolution, as the product of inexorable economic laws, is beyond the power of human beings either to prepare or to prevent (Kautsky dixit),[63] which is as good as saying it is ordained by God. As Lelio Basso has put it: 'Until her last breath, Rosa Luxemburg had faith in the victory of socialism, but she never grew tired of repeating that this victory would not be a matter of destiny, but the result of a stubborn and conscious battle on the part of the masses.'[64]

[62] See, for example, V. I. Lenin, *Collected Works,* Vol. 1, pp. 158, 174, 177–8; Vol. 21, p. 71.

[63] 'The Socialist party is a revolutionary party, but not a revolution-making party. We know that our goal can be attained only through a revolution. We also know that it is just as little in our power to create this revolution as it is in the power of our opponents to prevent it. It is no part of our work to instigate a revolution or to prepare the way for it.' K. Kautsky, *The Road to Power,* Chicago, 1909, p. 50.

[64] Basso, *loc. cit.*, p. 527.

Thirdly, the last cited passage from Luxemburg's work should in itself serve as sufficient warning that the mere presence in a text of formulations of this kind does not justify the imputation of fatalism. There it is written, black on white, that socialism is a historical necessity, the result of the very laws of capitalist development, *because* there is an alternative to it. What 'necessitates' it, i.e. makes it the indispensable means toward further historical progress, is the danger of universal ruin. There is more than one kind of necessity under the sun. Again, when Luxemburg speaks of revolutionary action as a way of accelerating a course of development which is in any case objectively in progress, she expresses ambiguously what is expressed perfectly adequately elsewhere in her work: namely, the view that Marxism fuses an interpretative theory, or science, of objective laws with the revolutionary energy and will, which, on the basis of that theory, attempt actually to change the world. The first divorced from the second, the theory from the practice, is not Marxism but a 'sad caricature', a 'miserable, rotten parody', of it.[65] This is recognisably the problematic of the *Theses on Feuerbach* and, as such, definitively distinct from any mechanistic conception of history.

In short, to accept at their face value the formulations in question, inferring from them, and against overwhelming evidence to the contrary, that Luxemburg's Marxism is economist, fatalist, spontaneist, is to denature the sense of her work. The conclusion of the foregoing argument is aptly summed up in the words, again, of Lelio Basso whose merit, unique to the best of our knowledge, is not only to have grasped the point (others have done that) but also to have expressed it clearly: 'When Rosa Luxemburg spoke of socialism as a historical necessity, she did not mean that she considered it a fatality.'[66] The judgement is borne out by these words from the last speech of her life: 'Socialism . . . [is] a historical necessity. Socialism is inevitable, not merely because proletarians are no longer willing to live under the conditions

[65] See above n. 20 and text.
[66] Basso, *loc. cit.*, p. 527.

imposed by the capitalist class, but further because, if the proletariat fails to fulfil its duties as a class, if it fails to realise socialism, we shall crash down together to a common doom.'[67]

In order to arrive at this conception in its broadest and most general lines, we have had to concern ourselves with the negative and preliminary task of clearing away the misunderstandings surrounding Luxemburg's breakdown theory which obscure it. In the third essay of this book, we shall undertake the more positive task of trying to illuminate the political concepts which define its content and make Luxemburg's rejection of the views with which she has so often been charged more than an abstract gesture. By way of conclusion here, we offer some observations on Luxemburg's notion of catastrophe.

*   *   *

'Proudhon . . . would formulate the *problem* thus: preserve the good side of this economic category, eliminate the bad. . . . For him the dialectic movement is the dogmatic distinction between good and bad. . . . What constitutes dialectical movement is the coexistence of two contradictory sides.' Karl Marx[68]

'There is one great fact, characteristic of this our Nineteenth Century. . . . On the one hand, there have started into life industrial and scientific forces, which no epoch of the former human history had ever suspected. On the other hand, there exist symptoms of decay, far surpassing the horrors recorded of the latter times of the Roman empire. In our days everything seems pregnant with its contrary.' Karl Marx[69]

It is beyond the purpose of this essay to pass judgement on the technical analysis which informs Luxemburg's theory of capitalist collapse. As far as we are competent to determine, it does seem to rest on a number of wrong assumptions concerning Marx's schemes of reproduction. Regardless of the

[67] 'Speech to the Founding Convention of the German Communist Party', Waters, p. 412.

[68] K. Marx, *The Poverty of Philosophy,* Moscow, 1966, p. 98.

[69] 'Speech at the Anniversary of the *People's Paper*', in K. Marx and F. Engels, *Selected Works,* 3 vols., Moscow, 1969, Vol. 1, p. 500.

economic analysis which founds it, however, it is not easy to make sense of the thesis that, independent of the struggle of the working class, capitalist economic relations must reach a point where their continued existence ceases to be possible, that capitalist society must then fall apart beyond all hope of repair. Such an idea, which has meaning with regard to a mechanical contraption or architectural structure, is misguided when applied to a set of social relations.[70] The same goes for the apocalyptic vision, implicit in that idea, of the end of civilisation and of society itself. No doubt, the prospect of nuclear and/or ecological catastrophe may, today, be invoked to lend that vision plausibility. But at any point short of extinction human society of one kind or another will oppose its imperatives to the putative threat of the void. Even the situation of endemic war, and of insoluble economic and political crises, which Luxemburg envisaged as the imperialist alternative to socialism, constitutes a mode of social existence with its own cultural forms, and not just irredeemable chaos.

That said, however, it would be a mistake simply to dismiss the socialism-or-barbarism formula as the product of a fevered imagination. For, it represents the extrapolation to its logical limit, *ad absurdum,* of something which is true and important, and which separates Marxism from all the philosophies of pure progress with which it has been confused. And that something is: the profoundly and inescapably contradictory nature of the whole of capitalist development. Imperialism, for Luxemburg, is not just the unbridled militarism and violence which allows her to speak of barbarism even before capitalism reaches its point of final collapse; it is also, as has already been said, the historical basis and material precondition of socialism.[71] Capitalism, throughout its course, is not only a series of technological and cultural achievements, an extension of political liberties and rights; it is also exploitation and repression, force, deceit and murder.[72] Luxemburg's

[70] Cf. Sweezy, *The Theory of Capitalist Development,* pp. 214–5.

[71] See, for example, 'Anti-Critique', p. 143, and 'The Junius Pamphlet', Waters, pp. 324–5.

[72] See, for example, *The Accumulation of Capital,* pp. 452–3, and 'Anti-Critique', p. 147.

perception of this is not limited to the innocent registration of an empirical fact, to the chronicling of a historical record. It is theoretically reflected in her conception of the very nature of capitalism, as the following quotation bears witness: 'It is one of the peculiarities of the capitalist order that within it all the elements of the future society first assume, in their development, a form not approaching socialism but, on the contrary, a form moving more and more away from socialism. . . . Exactly because capitalist development moves through these contradictions . . . must the proletariat seize political power and suppress completely the capitalist system . . . Social Democracy [does not attempt] the futile task of picking for itself all the good sides of history and rejecting the bad sides of history. . . . Capitalism furnishes besides the *obstacles* also the only *possibilities* of realising the socialist programme.'[73] To those like Bernstein, who wanted to free Marxism from its 'dialectical scaffolding', retaining only the emphasis on 'the growth of social wealth and of the social productive forces, in conjunction with general social progress',[74] capitalism is only recognisable in its good sides. The bad sides are arbitrary excrescences, warts on an otherwise lovely face. They are not integral to the existence of capitalism, and general social progress will in time remove them, or, more weakly, there is no reason in principle to prevent one thinking that they could be removed, to produce a 'pure', peaceful and democratic capitalist society. Those who nourish or purvey this hope have a long time to wait – 'roughly until the sun burns out' to borrow a phrase used by Luxemburg in a different context.

The celebrated contradiction between forces and relations of production is not fully understood if it is conceived, mechanistically, to refer only to a late or mature stage of capitalist development. Capitalist relations of production, on this conception, are progressive for a period because they foster the development of the productive forces; then, a point in time is reached when they cease to do this, act as

[73] 'Social Reform or Revolution', Waters, pp. 79–80.
[74] Bernstein, *op. cit.*, pp. 212–3.

fetters on the productive forces, come into conflict with them; only then does the contradiction arise. Making all due allowance for the truth expressed in this conception – that the achievements of capitalism are historically progressive and the essential pre-requisite for socialism – it is misleading, to say the least. For, this contradiction arises with the very origins of capitalism and is expressed in the fact that each of the latter's achievements, so long as it continues to serve capitalist ends, is double-edged. The advent of machinery was not an unmixed blessing to those who lived its effects; no more is technical innovation to the labouring population of contemporary capitalist societies. The scientific and technological development unleashed by capitalist society has provided not only increased forces of production and liberation but also new modes of destruction and oppression. It is sufficient to name them to uncover the 'rational kernel' in Luxemburg's vision of barbarism: gas chambers, nuclear weapons and napalm, 'scientific' methods of interrogation and torture, the free fire zone and the strategic hamlet. Capitalist society is not only parliamentary democracy and the rule of law but fascist dictatorship and police terror. All of which spells something other than unalloyed progress. If the limit of capitalism is a point in time, the point when its (living) victims will destroy it, it is equally something carried within that social order from its very inception – a congenital incapacity to subordinate its undoubted achievements to the needs of human beings; the human misery suffered and still being suffered; the unspeakable cruelties perpetrated and still being perpetrated in pursuance of its ends: exploitation and profit.

For this reason, it is quite incorrect to oppose to one another, as *alternative* characterisations of capitalism, the view that it is 'just the most recent form [of] slavery, in a broad sense of the word', and the view that it represents 'a progress', an important 'accretion of dignity, freedom and welfare for the masses of the people'.[75] Insofar as exploitation and the apparatus for its maintenance are realities, it is the first, and insofar

75 See G. A. Cohen, 'Remarks on Revolutionary Perspectives', *Radical Philosophy*, No. 2, Summer 1972, p. 23.

as the rule of law, trade unions, social security, better material and cultural standards, etc., *where these things exist at all,* represent significant gains, it is also the second. If to hold the first view to the exclusion of the second is to 'slur' the hard won achievements of the masses, then to hold the second to the exclusion of the first is to belittle their continued sufferings. Finally, the socialist revolution is neither simply 'a rupture with', nor simply 'a continuation of', all earlier human history. It is, in one and the same moment, or rather historical epoch, both the one and the other. It is of little account whether we borrow from Hegel and call it an *Aufhebung,* or whether, following countless lesser talents, we say: in certain relevant respects it is a continuation, in other relevant respects it is a rupture.

What is of some account is that we should not, blinded by capitalist progress, succumb to the religious and quasi-religious visions which make good present and past suffering by reference to future release from them. 'Even the ultimate advent of freedom cannot redeem those who died in pain.'[76]

---

[76] H. Marcuse, *Eros and Civilisation,* New York, 1961, p. 216.

Between the Russian Revolutions

As is well-known, a number of different strategic lines on the nature of the Russian revolution crystallised, during and immediately after 1905, out of a debate which received its impetus from the revolutionary upheaval of that year. Rosa Luxemburg was a participant in this debate within Russian and European Social Democracy. Her contribution is recorded in some of her articles and speeches of the period. These, and later writings, offer a coherent formulation of her general alignment in relation to the three contemporary conceptions provided, respectively, by the Mensheviks, by Lenin and by Trotsky. The present essay documents, and tries to resolve, the deep confusion which exists concerning Luxemburg's attitude toward the Russian revolution in the period before 1917.

I

In 1931, Stalin ventured a little essay in the historiography of the European socialist movement. Its main purpose was to assert that the struggle against Kautsky and the SPD 'centre' had been undertaken earlier and more energetically by Lenin than by Luxemburg and the German Left Social-Democrats. The opposite is in fact the truth: Luxemburg had been doing battle with SPD orthodoxy for nearly a decade when Lenin first became aware of its shortcomings; she broke with Kautsky in 1910, fully four years before the

SPD's response to the outbreak of war revealed to Lenin his own misappraisal of that party and its theoretical 'Pope'. In any case, in the course of denouncing this truth as a slander (to 'be branded as such and not made the subject of discussion'), Stalin also let it be understood that henceforth Rosa Luxemburg was to be regarded as one of the main architects of the theory of permanent revolution:

'In 1905, disagreement developed between the Bolsheviks and the Mensheviks in Russia on the question of the character of the Russian revolution. . . . What was the attitude of the German Left Social-Democrats, of Parvus and Rosa Luxemburg, to this controversy? They invented the utopian and semi-Menshevik (sic) scheme of permanent revolution . . . and opposed this scheme to the Bolshevik scheme of the revolutionary-democratic dictatorship of the proletariat and the peasantry. Subsequently, this semi-Menshevik scheme of permanent revolution was caught up by Trotsky . . . and transformed into a weapon of struggle against Leninism.'

Luxemburg's responsibility for inventing the theory and opposing it to the Bolshevik conception was ranked by Stalin amongst 'the most generally known facts of history'.[1] Wholly in keeping with the spirit of his essay, this was, however, less a comment on the differential epistemological status of various facts than something in the nature of the latest ultimatum. Six years earlier he had himself chastised the unfortunate Radek for allegedly attributing the same theory to Luxemburg. 'It is not true', Stalin had then written, 'that the theory of "permanent revolution" . . . was advanced in 1905 by Rosa Luxemburg and Trotsky. Actually, this theory was advanced by Parvus and Trotsky.'[2]

---

[1] 'Some Questions Concerning the History of Bolshevism' (1931), J. Stalin, *Leninism,* London, 1940, pp. 388–92.

[2] 'The October Revolution and the Tactics of the Russian Communists' (1924), *ibid.,* p. 101. The resolution of this contradiction was not beyond Stalin's talents. It seems that in 1905 Rosa Luxemburg invented the theory and opposed it to the Bolshevik conception without advancing it . . . against Lenin. Thus, according to Stalin (in 1932), the reticent Rosa 'kept behind the scenes in those days, abstained

Stalin's essay soon drew a reply from Trotsky himself. Having set the record straight with regard to Lenin's and Luxemburg's relationship to Kautsky before the First World War, Trotsky went on to deal with the authorship of the theory of permanent revolution. By now ascribing this to Luxemburg, he pointed out, Stalin was not only contradicting his own earlier assertion but also coming forward with a 'new' and 'unexpected history of the origin of the theory'. Trotsky also suggested, however, that Stalin's approach to historical questions, despite its vulgarity and unscrupulousness, had here generated a conclusion with a certain anachronistic rationale:

'[Stalin] approaches every question as if that question were born only today and stood apart from all other questions. [He] contributes his judgements entirely depending upon whatever personal interest of his is uppermost and most urgent today . . . Rosa Luxemburg does not appear to him in the perspective of the German, Polish, and international workers' movement of the last half-century. No, she is to him each time a new, and, besides, an isolated figure, regarding whom he is compelled in every . . . situation to ask himself anew, "Who goes there, friend or foe?" Unerring instinct has this time whispered to the theoretician of socialism in one country that the shade of Rosa Luxemburg is irreconcilably inimical to him.'[3]

The enmity postulated in this last assertion is by no means as speculative as the terminology may make it seem. Not only was Luxemburg's commitment to proletarian democracy quite incompatible with the practice of Stalinism. The consistent internationalism of her life and work was just as

---

from active struggle against Lenin in this matter, evidently preferring not to become involved as yet. . . . It was not Trotsky but Rosa Luxemburg and Parvus who *invented* the theory. . . . It was not Rosa Luxemburg but Parvus and Trotsky who in 1905 *advanced* [it] . . . *against* Lenin.' 'Reply to Olekhnovich and Aristov', J. Stalin, *Works,* Vol. 13, Moscow, 1955, pp. 133–4.

[3] 'Hands Off Rosa Luxemburg!', *Writings of Leon Trotsky 1932,* New York, 1973, pp. 139–41.

incompatible with the theory of socialism in one country.[4] More specifically, in assessing the significance of the Russian revolution *during and after 1917,* she did adopt a perspective essentially identical with Trotsky's theory of permanent revolution. Since Stalin was now writing in a context where, thanks to his own efforts, that theory existed in antagonistic relation to the idea of socialism in one country, he had good reason to detect a link between Luxemburg's political legacy and the Trotskyist opposition. With equally good reason Trotsky later placed the work of building the Fourth International 'under the sign of the "three L's", that is, not only under the sign of Lenin, but also of Luxemburg and Liebknecht'.[5] But of course all this leaves untouched the question of Luxemburg's connection with the theory of permanent revolution in the period before 1917. On that point, Trotsky, in his reply to Stalin, did no more than to register surprise and scepticism at her newly disclosed responsibility for its origin.

Elsewhere, however, he had himself connected her with the theory, albeit in a more limited way. At the Fifth Congress of the Russian Social-Democratic Party, held in London in May 1907, Trotsky noted that Luxemburg, in her interventions there, was espousing a view virtually indistinguishable from his own. Subsequently, referring to this occasion in his autobiography, he wrote: 'On the question of the so-called permanent revolution, Rosa took the same stand as I did.'[6] So expressed, even this more restricted claim is inaccurate. It is true that there was an important similarity between Luxemburg's and Trotsky's perspectives before 1917: both of them made the same assessment of the prole-

[4] Cf. V. Fay, Introduction to R. Luxemburg, *Lettres à Léon Jogichès,* 2 vols., Paris, 1971, Vol. 1, p. 12.

[5] 'Luxemburg and the Fourth International', *Writings of Leon Trotsky 1935–36,* New York, 1970, p. 112.

[6] L. Trotsky, *My Life,* New York, 1960, p. 203; and cf. L. Trotsky, *The Permanent Revolution & Results and Prospects,* London, 1962, p. 94. Nettl, though right to challenge the claim, is wrong to suggest that it was only made 'long after the actual events'. J. P. Nettl, *Rosa Luxemburg,* 2 vols., London, 1966, Vol. 2, p. 504 n. 1. On this, see below text for n. 86 of this essay.

tariat's leading role, and of its relationship to the other major classes, in the Russian revolution. Since much of the London Congress was devoted to a discussion of just that issue, it is also true that the common ground between them there was considerable and manifest. Trotsky's autobiographical contention, that Luxemburg's position at the Congress was the same as his own, undoubtedly refers to this area of overlap which was real enough. The claim is misleading, despite it, because before 1917 Rosa Luxemburg did not accept the central and decisive element in the theory of permanent revolution, the one which separated Trotsky from *all* of his contemporaries before 1917, not only from the Bolsheviks and the Mensheviks, but even from Parvus who genuinely had been instrumental in shaping Trotsky's thinking on the subject. She did not share Trotsky's view that the vanguard role of the proletariat in the Russian revolution would 'destroy the barriers between the minimum and maximum programme of Social Democracy', would forge 'an unbroken chain' between its bourgeois-democratic and socialist tasks, had therefore rendered obsolete the reigning orthodoxy of distinct and separate stages.[7] In this respect Luxemburg's views were more closely similar to Lenin's than to the theory of permanent revolution.

A legend to the contrary persists nevertheless and it is easy to see why. Stalin and Trotsky both laid the basis for it in different ways. Mutual antagonists in a comprehensive political and ideological confrontation which opposed them to one another on most things, they seemed at least to agree that she had had something to do with the theory in its early stages, whether by 'inventing' it or by endorsing it on one occasion shortly after its inception. Add to this that, in the last two years of her life, she did in effect endorse it, and a teleological reading of her work will do the rest. If one projects her later into her earlier conceptions, the partial similarity between these earlier conceptions and Trotsky's views can be taken for a simple identity. The operation is the more

---

[7] See *The Permanent Revolution & Results and Prospects,* pp. 163, 212, 8, 115–9.

tempting since certain of her formulations from the earlier period, if taken out of context, sound as if they might have been written by Trotsky. For example, in 1906, in her pamphlet on the mass strike, she characterised the Russian revolution 'not so much as the last successor of the old bourgeois revolutions as the forerunner of the new series of proletarian revolutions of the West'.[8] The sound here is deceptive precisely because it has been set loose from its place in Luxemburg's own orchestration. But it may help to account for the significant number of writers who, explicitly or implicitly, assimilate her perspective to Trotsky's theory of permanent revolution.

What they all have in common apart from being wrong, more accurately, the cause (or perhaps consequence) of their being wrong, is that they offer no detailed analysis of textual sources to substantiate the interpretation of Luxemburg they thereby make. Some simply make it in a general way without citing any sources.[9] Others make it by cursorily repeating the claim that she endorsed Trotsky's position at the London Congress.[10] Yet others do so by referring, without further analysis, to her pamphlet on the mass strike or to other writings of the same period.[11] As will be seen, these sources in

[8] 'The Mass Strike, the Political Party and the Trade Unions', M.-A. Waters (ed.), *Rosa Luxemburg Speaks*, New York, 1970, p. 203.

[9] K. Tarbuck, 'Biographical Notes' to R. Luxemburg and N. Bukharin, *Imperialism and the Accumulation of Capital*, London, 1972, pp. 2–3; H. Mehringer, 'Introduction historique' to L. Trotsky, *Nos Tâches Politiques*, Paris, 1970, pp. 15–18, 31ff.; L. Maitan, 'The Theory of Permanent Revolution', in E. Mandel (ed.), *Fifty Years of World Revolution*, New York, 1968, p. 57; M. Lowy, *Dialectique et Révolution*, Paris, 1973, p. 99.

[10] I. Deutscher, *The Prophet Armed*, London, 1954, p. 178; H. Schurer, 'The Russian Revolution of 1905 and the Origins of German Communism', *The Slavonic and East European Review*, Vol. 39, 1960–61, p. 467.

[11] R. Looker (ed.), *Rosa Luxemburg: Selected Political Writings*, London 1972, pp. 45–6; T. Cliff, *Rosa Luxemburg*, London, 1968, p. 14; C. Morgenstern, 'Trotsky et Rosa Luxemburg', *Quatrième Internationale*, No. 48, March 1971, pp. 22–3. Morgenstern also makes reference to Trotsky's claim concerning the London Congress. And cf. also L. Basso, *Rosa Luxemburg: A Reappraisal*, London, 1975, pp. 68–9, 79–81; Basso makes the same mistake, though quoting most of the sources which could have saved him from it.

Luxemburg's work fail when pursued. Here we simply take a closer look at one of the writers in question, by way of illustration. Robert Looker argues that 'As early as 1906 in her *Mass Strike* pamphlet, Luxemburg had rejected the schematic Menshevik view' – in which he is right – 'that Russia could as yet only hope to achieve a bourgeois revolution and that socialists must therefore confine their demands to the requirements of that revolution' – in which he is wrong, the above quotation from that pamphlet notwithstanding. What Rosa Luxemburg rejected about the Mensheviks' view was not the bourgeois-democratic objective of the Russian revolution but the strategic inferences they drew from this, such as the bourgeoisie's leading role, the necessity of an alliance with it, the desirability of supporting the Cadets, and so forth. Like Lenin, she disagreed with the Mensheviks about the methods necessary to win the most far-reaching demands consistent with the revolution's bourgeois character and not about this character itself. To make the same point differently, what Looker defines, inadequately, as the *Menshevik* view was in fact common to all Social-Democrats before 1917, except Trotsky and including Luxemburg. He thus helps to perpetuate the legend which assimilates the views of these two in that period.

On the other hand, a number of commentators have tried to demolish this legend by dissociating Luxemburg's views, explicitly or implicitly, from the theory of permanent revolution. But they invariably introduce new mistakes and confusions into the picture. One writer notes a theory of stages in her work before 1917 but, overlooking Trotsky, suggests that it was universal amongst Marxists at the time. Another correctly points to the same thing in her *Accumulation of Capital* but proceeds to deduce from it precisely the Menshevik variant, which Luxemburg rejected, of the need for 'an alliance with the national bourgeoisie'. A third suggests that she '*never* adopted the Trotskyist conception of permanent revolution', a suggestion sustained by the misconception that even the October Revolution effected no change of view on her part.[12] Nettl, whose account is the best, disputes the claim that she endorsed the theory of permanent revolution and draws attention to the fundamental solidarity between the Bolshevik view and her own. But he is mistaken in the qualification he makes to this by saying that in 1906 Luxemburg, unlike the Bolsheviks, did not 'talk of any dictatorship, either in words or by implication'.[13] She did talk, and in words, about a dictatorship: the dictatorship of the proletariat. She spoke of it as the only method of successfully carrying to completion the *bourgeois* revolution in Russia, and not, in Trotsky's sense, as the strategic objective whose achievement would fuse bourgeois-democratic and socialist tasks into one continuous revolutionary process. Finally, Ernest Mandel correctly stresses the bourgeois-democratic nature of the goal which she assigned to the revolutionary struggle of the Russian proletariat. But by writing that 'like Lenin, Luxemburg rejected as premature any attempt to establish the proletarian dictatorship in Russia', he makes the point in a way which obscures the precise contours of her position, and that for the reason just explained.[14]

There is, in sum, a more or less total confusion, and no clear and wholly accurate account known to us of Luxemburg's view in relation to those of her contemporaries.[15] What follows is an attempt to rectify this.

[12] Respectively: D. Howard (ed.), *Selected Political Writings of Rosa Luxemburg,* New York and London, 1971, p. 210; G. Lee, 'Rosa Luxemburg and the Impact of Imperialism', *The Economic Journal,* Vol. 81, No. 324, December 1971, pp. 852, 855–6, 858–9; V. Fay, *op. cit.,* Vol. 1, p. 29, emphasis added. On *The Accumulation of Capital,* see below text for n. 37 of this essay.

[13] Nettl, *op. cit.,* Vol. 1, pp. 90, 214, 338–9, 354–5; Vol. 2, pp. 504 n. 1, 553, 567. The mistaken qualification appears at p. 338: on this, see below text for n. 80 of this essay.

[14] E. Mandel, *The Leninist Theory of Organisation,* London, 1971, p. 22 n. 50.

[15] The account in P. Frölich, *Rosa Luxemburg* (London, 1972), is at best ambiguous and at worst inconsistent. It maintains, at different points, both that Luxemburg 'did not accept the idea of permanent revolution' (p. 122) and that 'In the most important questions concerning Russia she found herself in agreement with Trotsky' (p. 183). In general, it hovers uneasily between these alternatives. See pp. 19–21, 89–94, 109, 120–3.

II

Well before 1905 some general indications can be found in
Luxemburg's writings of the directions her thought would
take when brought to bear on the problems of the Russian
revolution. These are no more than indications. It was the
momentous events of 1905 itself which enabled her to con-
cretise them into a rounded out strategic perspective for
Russia. However, they already provide a clear anticipation of
what her response would be to the Menshevik 'orthodoxy' on
the Russian revolution: a blunt rejection of what she was to
refer to on one occasion as 'gigantic stupidities'.[16] Two such
anticipatory indications stand out in particular: Luxemburg's
assertion of the inherent prematurity of the proletarian
conquest of power; and the theme, pervading all her writings,
of the historical bankruptcy of bourgeois democracy and
liberalism.

The first was elaborated, at the turn of the century, against
Bernstein whose argument in favour of gradualism included
the notions that the proletariat was neither mature enough
to take power nor fit yet to wield it, and that the exercise of
proletarian power would in these circumstances be an impracticable, costly and disastrous experiment. The dictatorship of the proletariat, according to Bernstein, was, in a word,
premature, a most happy conclusion on his part seeing that
he deemed it to be ethically inadmissible in any case, since it
violated the norms of 'democracy' and, as such, belonged 'to
a lower civilisation . . . an age which did not know . . . the
present methods of the initiating and carrying of laws'.[17]
Luxemburg's retort was not limited to the observation that
beneath Bernstein's fears of a premature conquest of power
there lay in reality 'nothing more than a *general opposition to
the aspiration of the proletariat to possess itself of state power*'.
Examining the argument concerning prematurity on its own

---

[16] Letter to Emmanuel and Mathilde Wurm, 18/7/1906, cited in Frölich, *op. cit.*,
p. 124.
[17] E. Bernstein, *Evolutionary Socialism,* New York, 1961, pp. 146–7; and see
pp. 101–9, 155, 161–3, 196–7, 218–9.

terms, she also pointed out that it betrayed a mechanistic conception of the struggle for socialism to imagine that the necessary degree of proletarian political maturity could be produced or measured by factors extraneous to the class struggle itself, to the proletariat's struggle for, and exercise of, power and to the successes, failures and lessons of that whole process. Outside of the experience it provided there was no school of political maturity for the proletariat. For that reason, initiatives and even conquests of power which were, in a historical sense, premature would be unavoidable: 'These "premature" attacks of the proletariat constitute a factor, and indeed a very important factor, creating the political conditions of the final victory . . . in the course of the long and stubborn struggles, the proletariat will acquire the degree of political maturity permitting it to obtain in time a definitive victory of the revolution.' It should be borne in mind, however, that Luxemburg's argument here was developed in the context of a controversy about the general strategic orientation of the German SPD and justifies neither the inference that she believed socialist revolution to be on the agenda *everywhere and immediately,* nor the imputation to her of *tactical* recklessness. Her contention was simply that the proletariat's struggle for power could not be postponed until it was completely assured, in advance, of a definitive victory in ideal conditions, since that would be a postponement *sine die.* No revolution could even begin if its precondition was the complete political maturity of the proletariat, and no conquest of power be undertaken if it had to be legitimated by guarantees of perfect success. Where the conditions for the revolutionary seizure of power emerged, the proletariat could and must, nevertheless, attempt, within the limits of its strength, to implement its historical objectives. 'There can be no time', Luxemburg wrote, 'when the proletariat, placed in power by the force of events, is not in the condition . . . to take certain measures for the realisation of its programme.'[18]

[18] 'Social Reform or Revolution', Waters, pp. 81–3.

The significance of this argument in the present context and its distance from simple 'rebel's impatience'[19] are revealed by a consideration of the second theme, Luxemburg's diagnosis of the contemporary condition and prospects of bourgeois democracy. The programme of German Social Democracy, adopted at Erfurt in 1891, contained not only those demands, the so-called maximum programme, in which the party expressed its ultimate, socialist objective, but also a set of immediate demands – the minimum programme, to be fought for and won on the terrain of capitalist society itself – concerning the acquisition and extension of bourgeois rights and liberties and the improvement of the material conditions of the working class. Luxemburg's attitude to the minimum programme was far from being cavalier, despite her sustained fight against the way in which it was understood and projected, first by the revisionists, then by the party leadership and the political 'centre' from which the leadership drew its support. She vigorously opposed the revisionist attempt to excise the maximum programme from the perspectives of the SPD. From 1905 onwards she opposed, equally vigorously, the party's actual practice of delaying the struggle for socialism to some unspecified future even while continuing to affirm and reaffirm its currency. She tirelessly exposed as illusory and false the conceptions on which this contradictory practice was based: that the trade-unionist and parliamentary struggle for the minimal demands could be a substitute for a strategy of mass struggle leading towards the conquest of power; that secreted within that day-to-day, bread-and-butter struggle was some automatic trajectory towards socialism; that the trade-union and electoral strength of the working class could 'become', through organic growth and a Social-Democratic majority in the Reichstag, the dictatorship of the proletariat; that bourgeois parliamentarism itself might be the organ of proletarian dictatorship and democracy. Yet, at no time and in no way did Luxemburg belittle the importance

---

[19] Kautsky's later characterisation of Luxemburg's positions. See C. E. Schorske, *German Social Democracy 1905–1917,* New York, 1970, p. 185.

to be attached to the struggle of the working class for elementary bourgeois-democratic rights. She believed, on the contrary, that that struggle was now the '*only* support' capable of sustaining bourgeois democracy, and that one of Social Democracy's most urgent contemporary tasks was 'to save bourgeois parliamentarism from the bourgeoisie'.[20]

Underlying this belief were two arguments, both of them expressed during the course of the revisionist controversy, though Luxemburg continued to adhere to them thereafter. The first was that the institutions of bourgeois democracy, albeit no substitute for the dictatorship of the proletariat which they could not render superfluous, were needed by the working class nevertheless, since the rights of organisation and expression which they allowed, and the very struggle for the defence and enlargement of those rights, constituted at least part of the indispensable preparation for its conquest, and exercise, of power. The second was that these same institutions of bourgeois democracy had, from the point of view of the bourgeoisie, exhausted their historical function and would be, indeed were being, progressively abandoned by it. Luxemburg challenged Bernstein's naive and unilinear view according to which some law of progress guaranteed that democracy was the exclusive or even natural political form for capitalist relations of production, all other reactionary political phenomena being no more than accidental aberrations from the general law. Not only was this false historically, since capitalism had already coexisted with numerous political forms, from absolute monarchy through constitutional monarchy and democratic republic to Bonapartism. It also provided a dangerously mystifying perspective for the future. Bourgeois democracy, according to Luxemburg, had played a necessary though limited historical role in the bourgeoisie's struggle against feudalism and in its mobilisation of the masses in that cause. But so soon as this struggle was completed or compromised, so soon as its 'stimulating fire' went out, as she

[20] 'Social Reform or Revolution', Waters, p. 76; 'Social Democracy and Parliamentarianism', Looker, p. 110.

contended it had already done on a more or less international scale, then bourgeois democracy lost its historical purpose, became useless and dispensable to the bourgeoisie itself. Threatened by a rising working class and racked by the convulsions of imperialist rivalry and militarism, the bourgeoisie would not hesitate to jettison its own democratic institutions. Since these had now lost the kind of support provided by this class in its 'heroic' period, Luxemburg's prognosis for them, should the workers' movement fail in their defence, was uniformly bleak. Hence the assertions that 'democratic institutions . . . have completely exhausted their function as aids in the development of bourgeois society', that 'liberalism . . . is now absolutely useless to bourgeois society', that 'bourgeois democracy must logically move in a descending line', that 'bourgeois parliamentarism has . . . completed the cycle of its historical development and has arrived at the point of self-negation', that 'parliamentarism has lost all significance for capitalist society'.[21]. Hence the references, in a later period, to 'the inner wretchedness of bourgeois liberalism', to the 'merciless trampling down of the last remnants of . . . bourgeois liberalism and bourgeois progress', to 'the miserable breakdown of the last remnants of . . . bourgeois democracy'.[22]

There is in all this an evident underestimation on Luxemburg's part of bourgeois democracy's potential use, to the capitalist class, and potential life span, as one form of capitalist rule, within the metropolitan centres of imperialism. It should first be said, however, that her whole conception was in no respect inferior, neither analytically nor predictively, to the rosy Bernsteinian vision, an essentially liberal one, against which it was directed. She understood that the bourgeoisie would nowhere again be prepared to wage, let alone lead, an energetic revolutionary fight for the democratic objectives of the bourgeois revolution. She recognised that there were no

[21] 'Social Reform or Revolution', Waters, pp. 56, 73–6, 80–1; 'Social Democracy and Parliamentarianism', Looker, pp. 106–10.
[22] 'What Now?', Looker, p. 172; 'The Idea of May Day on the March', Howard, p. 318.

lengths, howsoever undemocratic, to which it would not go in defence of its rule and in pursuit of imperialist ambitions. She grasped earlier and better than anyone else that the European working class had reached a historical turning point, that the epoch of peaceful growth and struggle in the context of capitalist stability lay behind it, while ahead there stretched a period of economic crisis and violent political conflict. Her writings can be seen as one long effort to erect a signpost at that turning point in order to save the working class from misdirection on a new terrain. When the policy of the SPD which she had criticised for a decade came to fruition, during the First World War, in the *Burgfrieden* and the party's support for the 'Fatherland', she anticipated the general essence, if not the precise and convulsive forms, of the unparalleled calamity which this capitulation foreshadowed and which, twenty years later, would overtake the German and European working class and European Jewry in the shape of triumphant Nazism. In 1915 Luxemburg wrote the following prescient lines:

'German freedom . . . has been endangered by this attitude of the Social Democracy far beyond the period of the present war. The leaders of the Social Democracy are convinced that democratic liberties for the working class will come as a reward for its allegiance to the fatherland. But never in the history of the world has an oppressed class received political rights as a reward for service rendered to the ruling classes. . . . The indifference with which the German people have allowed themselves to be deprived of the freedom of the press, of the right of assembly and of public life, the fact that they not only calmly bore, but even applauded the state of siege is unexampled in the history of modern society. . . . That such a thing is possible in Germany today, that not only the bourgeois press, but the highly developed and influential socialist press as well, permits these things without even the pretence of opposition bears a fatal significance for the future of German liberty. It proves that society in Germany today has within itself no foundation for political freedom, since it allows itself to be thus lightly deprived of its most sacred rights. Let us not forget that the political rights that existed in Germany before the war were not won, as were those of France and England, in great and repeated revolutionary struggles, are not firmly anchored in the lives of the people by the power of revolutionary tradition. They are the gift of a Bismarckian policy granted after a period of victorious counter-revolution that lasted over twenty years. German liberties did not ripen on the field of revolution, they are the product of diplomatic gambling by Prussian military monarchy, they are the cement with which this military monarchy has united the present German empire. Danger threatens the free development of German freedom not . . . from Russia, but in Germany itself. It lies in the peculiar counter-revolutionary origin of the German constitution, and looms dark in the reactionary powers that have controlled the German state since the empire was founded. . . . The passive submission of the Social Democracy to the present state of siege . . . has demoralised the masses, the only existing pillar of German constitutional government.'[23]

Judged against a period which was bracketed by two bloody and destructive world wars, a period in which bourgeois democracy, where it survived, was subject to severe strain and pressure and, where it did not, made way for the most murderous variant of capitalist rule, Luxemburg's forecasts concerning the destiny of bourgeois democracy in the advanced countries are actually remarkable in one sense for their perspicacity. Nor is it entirely surprising if she did not see beyond this grim and extended reality to the era of renewed capitalist stabilisation and expansion which followed it and in which bourgeois democracy was better able to prove its capacity for survival and revival. Theoretically, of course, her conception of capitalist accumulation precluded the possibility of such economic recovery, predicating an increasing aggravation of the problem of realising surplus-value on the

---

[23] 'The Junius Pamphlet', Waters, pp. 297–9.

shrinkage of the non-capitalist environment. But there is a more important point here. Historically, capitalist recovery, after 1945, was in part the product of the preceding series of massive and repeated defeats for the European working class. No Marxist of Luxemburg's generation could fully foresee or measure them, much less all their effects, before the First World War, even though in her own case the onset of the war provided her with an inkling of their possibility. It may be added that that recovery could, in any case, be no more lasting or permanent than the period which produced a Bernstein, for all that it too, at its peak, spawned its own soothing myths. The stability enjoyed by advanced capitalism after the Second World War has already, and quite visibly, begun to fracture.

Even now, however, bourgeois democracy is far from being useless to the bourgeoisie. Luxemburg's early admonition of its demise in favour of more reactionary variants of capitalist rule, her failure to appreciate its potential resilience in the major countries of developed capitalism, must also partly be put down to a somewhat unilateral definition of its historical role: her belief that it was a political form specific to the bourgeoisie's struggle against feudalism. In fact, it is a form which has shown itself to be sturdiest where, and in the measure that, that struggle has been consummated,[24] a form of the bourgeoisie's consolidated ascendency and not merely of its fight for it. From the point of view of the bourgeoisie there are excellent reasons for giving this political form its support. Bourgeois democracy performs the function, a not so heroic one this, of securing and maintaining the consent of the masses to their own exploitation and subordination. This point should not be oversimplified but nor can it be evaded. In a polemical observation, which may appear to contradict the bald manner in which it is here expressed, Trotsky once wrote for example: 'Anyone who would say that in England, France, the United States, and other democratic countries, private property is supported by the will of the people would be a

[24] As the last quoted passage indicates, Luxemburg herself was aware of this. It did not, however, restrain her from statements, of the kind noted above, which across all national histories declared bourgeois democracy to be generally moribund.

liar. No one ever asked the consent of the people.'[25] The truth of this observation is that bourgeois democracy obtains the consent of the masses not by revealing their subordination to them, but by concealing it from them, much as the wage form conceals the existence of their exploitation. It throws up a screen (which is not just a fiction, however, but a real structure with real effects) of elections, parliamentary legislation and debate, equal democratic rights, etc., behind which the central, executive apparatuses of the state and their points of contact/access to the capitalist class are obscured. It thus creates the illusion in the masses that they control this democratic state at least as much as anybody else. What they consent to is not something which they know to be their own subordination in the light of the clearly presented historical alternative of its abolition but a structure which they understand quite otherwise. A kind of consent is secured from them nevertheless, even if it is misguided and misinformed, even if it is never entirely perfect from the point of view of the capitalist class, because pierced by the experience of a rather less benign reality, contradictory, and therefore in need of reinforcement by the constant threat, and periodic use, of violence.

Trotsky himself understood this. He explained it clearly in a series of writings on Germany embodying not only brilliant, and still unsurpassed, conjunctural analyses of the rise of Nazism, but also the elements of a theory of the capitalist state not to be found in the previous Marxist canon, not in Marx, nor in Lenin, nor in Luxemburg, and one which, to this day, has not been properly assimilated in Marxist research – less still by the most influential currents within the workers' movement. One of Trotsky's main concerns in these writings was precisely to elucidate the different forms and methods of bourgeois rule and the different social blocs they attempt to construct, and lean on, for their support. On the subject of bourgeois democracy he wrote: 'In a developed capitalist society, during a "democratic" regime, the bourgeoisie leans for support primarily upon the working classes, which are

---

[25] *Leon Trotsky on Britain,* New York, 1973, p. 72.

held in check by the reformists. In its most finished form, this system finds its expression in Britain during the administration of the Labour government as well as during that of the Conservatives.'[26]

Bourgeois democracy's strength in eliciting such support derives from mechanisms of ideological legitimation and political integration incomparably more powerful than those available to the alternative, overtly repressive forms of bourgeois rule and for want of which the latter employ systematic terror. All bourgeois democracies, to be sure, also possess an armed, repressive apparatus which they use not only as a last resort, when these other mechanisms begin to fail decisively, but also on a more regular basis: piecemeal or in generous doses depending on the nature of the case. They rely upon 'a combination of repressions and concessions'.[27] But the basic pillar of their strength is a dense and complex structure of institutions and practices, many of them external to the state apparatus itself – of elections, legislative, executive and advisory bodies, political parties, pressure groups and trade unions, newspapers and other mass media, etc. – through which the needs and demands of the masses are processed. This structure has a dual character. On the one hand, it does provide the workers' movement with the organisational and political means for opposing the more blatant forms of exploitation and oppression, for defending the workers' most immediate interests, and for winning material gains on their behalf. This provision is the source of bourgois democracy's self-legitimating power, and explains why it is no *mere* fraud and why an attitude of sectarian, ultra-left abstentionism towards it will not win the confidence of politically conscious workers. On the other hand, this structure largely succeeds in sublimating and neutralising, or sabotaging, such genuinely anti-capitalist demands and initiatives as do emerge, by taking them through its many 'competent' and 'specialised' channels, i.e., away from the masses, out of their direct control

[26] L. Trotsky, *The Struggle Against Fascism in Germany*, New York, 1971, p. 158.
[27] *ibid.*, p. 281.

and sight – generally with the assistance of reformist workers' parties and trade-union leaders. This is why bourgeois democracy is *in large measure* a fraud, not class-neutral, not democratic *tout court,* and why the purely parliamentary road to socialism is a vain hope. The costs of this type of polity to the bourgeoisie, costs attendant on not having a prostrate workers' movement at its command, are not to be denied. But it has often been prepared to bear them, especially in the advanced countries where it could most afford to. Their levels of wealth and position within the imperialist nexus made possible, over long periods, fundamental concessions to the working class in terms of rising standards of living.

From the point of view of the bourgeoisie there are also certain risks. The organisational strength which the working class is able to build up can become a serious threat to bourgeois rule once it begins to be released in the direction of forms of proletarian self-activity and self-organisation which over-flow bourgeois democracy's constricting framework and paralyse its function as the political expropriator of the initiatives of the masses. Bourgeois democracy *itself* furnishes points of support from which such initiatives toward proletarian democracy and power can be launched. This is why abstentionism is also a miserable substitute for a socialist strategy which can learn how to use these points of support in a revolutionary way, opening up the contradiction within bourgeois democracy in order to dispatch it once and for all. The bourgeoisie has, in any case, been prepared to live with these risks up to a point. But only up to a point. Wherever and whenever the dam has begun to burst, it has moved, in the most resolute and bloodiest possible fashion, to liquidate all the paraphernalia of democratic government; and no one has yet produced a convincing reason for thinking that things are now different in this respect, though before 11 September 1973 Chile was offered in place of a reason. Luxemburg was therefore entirely correct to insist that the capitalist class is *everywhere* less sentimental about democracy than about its own continued rule. Nor was she alone in doing so. It has been a central principle of revolutionary Marxism, supported by good evidence, that the road to socialism cannot bypass the preparation of the working class and its allies for armed self-defence and armed struggle. Accordingly, the denial of this principle by individuals and organisations within the labour movement, whether Social-Democratic or Communist, has always marked their passage toward, or destination at, a meliorative, reformist perspective unable to get beyond or, sometimes, even see beyond the end of capitalist society.

None of this, however, adds up to bourgeois democracy's uselessness to the bourgeoisie in an epochal sense. It is not just that it has proved its worth, in certain conditions and over a considerable period of time, as a means of containing and integrating the masses. The course of liquidating it into naked repression, particularly where it has achieved any real hold, also entails both risks and costs for the bourgeoisie. For, this course amounts to an open declaration of war on the workers' movement, a war whose outcome is never entirely certain. Even if the bourgeoisie triumphs, this is likely to be at the expense of a profound economic dislocation, and of a general-ised ideological and social crisis which it will not quickly be able to repair. Furthermore, the hands into which it thereby entrusts its rule, whether those of military chieftains or those of fascist demagogues, have not always proved as pliable to its will or as sensitive to the long-term dictates of capitalist accumulation as have its democratic representatives and functionaries. It is out of fears and considerations of this kind that the bourgeoisie, though often forced to resort to them, is less than enthusiastic about what Trotsky, in a reference to fascism, termed 'the "plebeian" means of solving its prob-lems'.[28] While, therefore, there is every reason, both defensive and offensive, for the workers' movement to be alert and vigorous in its attention to bourgeois democracy, a point on which Luxemburg was, once again, perfectly correct to insist, it is not true to suggest, as she did, that the bourgeoisie for its part will carelessly or lightmindedly abandon it. By the same token, it is not universally true to say that the workers' move-

[28] *ibid.*, p. 282.

ment is its *only* contemporary support. On the contrary, where the workers' movement is the only such support, there bourgeois democracy is doomed in a much shorter term sense than Luxemburg intended, frequently a conjunctural one. Withdrawing its support from democratic institutions which are beginning to jeopardise its rule, the bourgeoisie will either succeed in finding the means to overturn them or it will fail, and if it fails in *that* then the ultimate sanctions of its hegemony will have crumbled. The working class will understand this.

The capitalist class, to conclude here, has continued to give support to bourgeois democracy in certain conditions not because this class is, in the Twentieth Century, a revolutionary or progressive force, but because it is not. It has used bourgeois democracy, where it could, to arrest that one form of revolutionary progress which has been haunting it for over a century and which is now more urgent than ever, the emancipation of the working masses from exploitation. Bourgeois democracy still performs this function for it in the countries of advanced capitalism today. How long it can continue to do so is a problem that has yet to be resolved.

III

Luxemburg's underestimation of bourgeois democracy's potential resilience in the advanced capitalist countries was coupled with a converse, and paradoxical, overestimation of its prospects outside those countries – in particular, of its prospects in Russia. This complement was paradoxical because the force which she herself posited as having been the precondition for the birth of a bourgeois-democratic polity was, on her own analysis, absent from the Russian situation. Here there was no bourgeois class ready to undertake, in a spirit of democratic radicalism and at the head of the workers and peasants, a resolute fight against the Tsarist order. What served to give this paradox at least a semblance of coherence in her work was the theme, discussed above, that

bourgeois democracy's unique support was now the proletariat itself. This theme, in fact, was the copula linking
Luxemburg's differential prognoses for the different environ-
ments. In the advanced countries the workers were to keep
bourgeois democracy alive against the opposition of a bourgeoisie which had deserted it. What life it had left in it was
entirely due to this proletarian sustenance which meant that
it would henceforth function less as a stable form of bourgeois
rule, in which capacity it was becoming increasingly useless,
than as a weapon in the struggle for socialism. In Russia, on
the other hand, this same struggle could not yet be on the
agenda. The Russian workers' movement was separated from
any attempt to implement the goals of the maximum programme by a whole historical stage, one of further capitalist
development and of bourgeois-democratic rule during which
it would be strengthened both numerically and politically.
Here bourgeois democracy had still to begin its life. But here
too it had been deserted, forsworn even as an aspiration
before it could become a reality, by a bourgeoisie which was
heavily compromised with the old order and fearful of the
consequences of sanctioning any mass revolutionary movement. In Russia, therefore, the proletariat would have
actually to create bourgeois democracy against the opposition
of the bourgeoisie.

All the elements of this perspective are already present in
Luxemburg's writings before 1905, as can be seen from a text
of 1903 on the antecedents of Polish Social Democracy. It is
directed against certain Blanquist and populist illusions in the
ideological positions of the Polish Proletariat Party of the
1880s, a circumstance whose importance will be considered
in due course. In it, Luxemburg insists that the proletarian
'revolution is impossible if the bourgeois society has not
previously passed through the necessary phases of development', if it has not 'already reached a state of economic as well
as political development which allows the introduction of
socialist institutions'. The 'indispensable stage in the development of . . . capitalist society' which she has most in mind is
that of 'parliamentary-bourgeois forms of government', and

she condemns as Blanquist the hope of 'carrying out a socialist overthrow directly, without going through the bourgeois-parliamentary phase'.[29] Accordingly, she upholds for the Russian Empire, including Congress Poland, the distinction between the minimum and the maximum programmes, and rejects any notion that a programme of measures *transitional* towards socialism might there be applicable.[30] The decisive current goal is specified and reiterated as 'the winning of political freedom, i.e., constitutional forms within Russia', as 'the overthrow of personal rule and the struggle for political freedom and a parliamentary-democratic form of government'. At the same time, Luxemburg is already clear which class will have to shoulder the burden of this struggle: 'The attaining of democratic institutions in the state . . . is – at a certain historical moment, in a certain phase in the development of class antagonism – impossible without the active struggle of a conscious and organised proletariat.'[31]

Before 1905, in other words, Luxemburg subscribed to the Social-Democratic orthodoxy according to which 'the revolution soon to break out in Russia will be a bourgeois and not a proletarian revolution'.[32] Even then, however, she was not prepared to deduce from this that it must be led by the political representatives of the bourgeoisie, a deduction the Mensheviks would not hesitate to make. As logical as it may have seemed to them to be, it did violence to the reality of the Russian situation and to Luxemburg's sense of that reality. 'In Russia', she had written in 1899, 'capitalism prospered for a long time under the regime of oriental absolutism, without having the bourgeoisie manifest the least desire in the world to introduce democracy.'[33]

The revolution of 1905 itself preserved the outlines of this perspective intact, as regards both the putative objective of

[29] 'In Memory of the Proletariat Party', Howard, pp. 179–80, 206, 202.

[30] *ibid.*, pp. 193–6. The text is very clear on this point. Dick Howard misunderstands the meaning of a 'transitional programme' when he suggests (p. 163) that this is what it argues for.

[31] *ibid.*, pp. 185, 187, 180.

[32] 'Organisational Questions of Russian Social Democracy', Waters, p. 127.

[33] 'Social Reform or Revolution', Waters, p. 74.

the Russian revolution and the roles within it of bourgeoisie and proletariat respectively. The political weakness and vacillation of Russian liberalism, on the one hand, and the enormous revolutionary energy of the Russian workers, on the other, were both features of 1905 which confirmed to Luxemburg's mind the correctness of her general position. But the events of that year also enabled her to give concreteness and precision to what had hitherto been a merely indicative and rather abstract schema, because they provided her with the raw materials out of which to fashion clearer strategic ideas about the exact dimensions of the proletariat's role. These raw materials were the forms of struggle embraced by the Russian masses themselves. In the vast wave of mass strikes and demonstrations which flowed over the Russian Empire during 1905, Luxemburg perceived the methods of assault which would be required to bring Tsarism to its knees and which, in order to do this and in the course of doing it, would sensitise the masses to the intimate connection between their economic and political problems, would foster and strengthen the forms of their self-organisation, would impart to them an invaluable and irreplaceable lesson in the practice of proletarian democracy, and would prepare the most fertile ground for the implantation of revolutionary socialist ideas. Moreover, she understood the truly international significance of this whole experience. The Russian workers had, she held, adopted forms of struggle which were more advanced, more effective and more specifically proletarian in character than those to which the European workers' movement had become accustomed, schooled as this was in years of peaceful, parliamentary and trade-unionist activity. They had furnished an example to the international working class which it would have to assimilate and repeat wherever it embarked upon any decisive struggle for power. To be adequately prepared and oriented for such a struggle, the European workers' parties and leaders must learn from the Russian workers, which meant in particular that the limitations of the 'good old', 'tried and tested', parliamentary tactic of the SPD must now be recognised. Luxemburg's grasp of this point was second to no one's.[34] And it was in this sense, and this sense alone, that she spoke about the Russian revolution, in formulations which have led many commentators astray, as the forerunner of the proletarian revolutions of the West, as having 'a more pronounced proletarian class-character than any previous revolution', as being 'a pure proletarian one'.[35] What she meant was not that the Russian proletariat could now go beyond the objectives of the bourgeois revolution but that, in order even to reach them, it had already begun, in advance and anticipation of the European proletariat, to extend and deepen the forms of proletarian combat, and would have to pursue this course to the maximum limit: to the point indeed where – as the ultimate consequence of the Luxemburgist paradox – it would *temporarily* hold state power in its hands.

It is here precisely that we arrive at the fusion, within Luxemburg's response to 1905, of the two themes treated in Section II of this essay: the world-historical bankruptcy of bourgeois democracy and the irreducible prematurity of the proletarian conquest of power. According to her, the flight of the bourgeoisie from its own liberal values and institutions into the arms of counter-revolution meant, in a country like Russia which had yet to experience the most elementary benefits of bourgeois democracy, that the dictatorship of the proletariat would be required to secure them. In a broad historical sense, that dictatorship would be premature because unable, in the objective conditions defined by the Russian social formation, to initiate a transition to socialism. However, to the Menshevik fears of such prematurity Luxemburg opposed the view that, if the Russian proletariat was bound to suffer a defeat of sorts by having to give up the power which it would for a time possess, this had to be measured against the considerations that the proletariat in power would do its

[34] This is not just a rhetorical flourish. Neither Lenin nor Trotsky, it is true, overlooked the international significance of the Russian revolution of 1905. However, as regards the urgency, signalled by 1905, of a major strategic reorientation by European, and especially German, Social Democracy, Luxemburg's thinking was in advance of theirs. It is this, as much as her closer acquaintance with Kautsky, which enabled her to perceive the signs of the latter's renegacy earlier than they did.

[35] See above text for n. 8, and below text for n. 78, of this essay.

best to implement the entire minimum programme of Social Democracy[36] and that the goals embodied in that programme, themselves indispensable preconditions of the struggle for socialism, could not otherwise be reached – certainly not by heeding the Menshevik advice concerning the need for 'tact' and circumspection toward the liberals, the need, that is, to *restrict* the scope of proletarian struggle and subordinate it to the timid initiatives of the Cadets so as not to antagonise them. Luxemburg's perspective, therefore, remained locked within the problematic of a path to socialism involving two distinct, and chronologically separate, revolutionary stages, the first bourgeois, the second proletarian, in aim. It was, for all that, different in a decisive respect from the outlook of the Mensheviks. In 1917, her alignment was to be determined by that decisive difference rather than by the stages theory, hitherto common to her and them, which she finally, but definitively, discarded.

Right up until 1917, however, this theory continued to inhabit her work. It is evident, for example, in the following passage from *The Accumulation of Capital,* published in 1913, in which the Russian revolution, though its proletarian features are alluded to, is situated firmly within a schema of *capitalist* emancipation from imperialist domination: 'The achievement of capitalist autonomy in the *hinterland* and backward colonies is attained amidst wars and revolutions. Revolution is an essential for the process of capitalist emancipation. The backward communities must shed their obsolete political organisations, relics of natural and simple commodity economy, and create a modern state machinery adapted to the purposes of capitalist production. The revolutions in Turkey, Russia and China fall under this heading. The last two, in particular, do not exclusively serve the immediate political requirements of capitalism; to some extent they carry over outmoded pre-capitalist claims while on the other hand they already embody new conflicts which run counter to the domination of capital. These factors account for their

[36] Cf. above text for notes 18 and 19 of this essay.

immense drive, but at the same time impede and delay the ultimate victory of the revolutionary forces. A young state will usually sever the leading strings of older capitalist states by wars, which temper and test the modern state's capitalist independence in a baptism by fire. That is why military together with financial reforms invariably herald the bid for economic independence.'[37] Again, in 1915, discussing the failure of 1905, Luxemburg characterises the Russian revolution in these terms: 'There was the difficulty . . . of creating a class state for the supremacy of the modern bourgeoisie against the counter-revolutionary opposition of the bourgeoisie as a whole. . . . It was a proletarian revolution with bourgeois duties and problems, or if you wish, a bourgeois revolution waged by socialist proletarian methods.'[38]

Torn from this last quotation the phrase, 'proletarian revolution with bourgeois duties and problems', can of course be read in a Trotskyist sense, since for Trotsky the Russian revolution did have bourgeois problems to resolve:[39] its 'permanence' signified not the simple circumvention ('leaping', in the Stalinist terminology) of these problems, but their inseparable *combination* with properly socialist tasks. Enough has already been said to indicate why such a reading of Luxemburg's phrase would be incorrect and, in context, its meaning is in any case unambiguous: proletarian in method, the Russian revolution is nevertheless bourgeois in content, its objective being the consolidation of the political supremacy of the modern bourgeoisie.[40] In Section IV of this essay, we shall document at greater length, and by direct reference to

[37] R. Luxemburg, *The Accumulation of Capital*, London, 1963, p. 419.

[38] 'The Junius Pamphlet', Waters, p. 290.

[39] Cf. for example: 'The democratic tasks of backward Russia . . . could be achieved only through a dictatorship of the proletariat'; and 'The application of *socialist* methods for the solution of *pre-socialist* problems – that is the very essence of the present economic and cultural work in the Soviet Union.' L. Trotsky, *The Revolution Betrayed*, New York, 1965, pp. 5, 57.

[40] As another representative of Polish Social Democracy put it in 1908: 'The proletariat has to impose its own solution . . . by reaching a class dictatorship, by capturing the heights of power in order to lift up and help to extend the power of its own eventual antagonists, the bourgeoisie.' Cited in Nettl, *op. cit.*, Vol. 2, p. 567.

her statements during and immediately after 1905, Luxemburg's attachment to the perspective which has here been briefly sketched.

Before doing that, we want to situate this perspective in the context of the wider controversy of which it was a part and to uncover some of its theoretical assumptions and implications. In particular, reference will be made to Lenin's writings of the period, for, with certain differences of emphasis, his strategic orientation was broadly the same as Luxemburg's. Fifty years of uninterrupted obfuscation on the part of all those currents in the socialist movement which trace their lineage back, in one way and another, through Stalin, have succeeded in blurring the exact nature of the differences that divided the various parties to the controversy over the Russian revolution. Since the object of this essay is to give a clear account of Luxemburg's position within that debate, some clarification of the issues at stake in it is essential; otherwise, the explanation of her work here being attempted may simply be lost in the broader confusion. We shall take as our point of departure for this discussion a number of passages in which Lenin, in the period 1906–9, invokes the authority of Kautsky in support of the strategic perspective of the Bolsheviks.[41]

'Is the revolution in Russia a bourgeois or a socialist revolution? That is not the way to put the question, says Kautsky. . . . Of course, the Russian revolution is not a socialist revolution. The socialist dictatorship of the proletariat (its "undivided sway") is out of the question. But neither is it a bourgeois revolution, for *"the bourgeoisie is not one of the driving forces of the present revolutionary movement in Russia"*. "Wherever the proletariat comes out independently, the bourgeoisie

---

[41] The Kautsky of 1905–6 was not the same political animal as the Kautsky who in 1917–8 wrote *The Dictatorship of the Proletariat*. In particular, it would be a mistake to infer from his hostile response to the October Revolution, which aligned him with the Mensheviks, that he shared their position in the earlier period. As is evident from what follows, he did not, for at this time he was politically close to Rosa Luxemburg.

ceases to be a revolutionary class." . . . This first answer of Kautsky's is a brilliant vindication of the fundamental principles of Bolshevik tactics. . . . To interpret the category "bourgeois revolution" in the sense of recognising the leadership and guiding role of the bourgeoisie in the Russian revolution is to vulgarise Marxism.'

'The revolution in Russia is not a socialist revolution, for it *cannot possibly* result in the *sole* rule or dictatorship of the proletariat. . . . A bourgeois revolution, brought about by the proletariat and the peasantry in spite of the instability of the bourgeoisie – this fundamental principle of Bolshevik tactics is wholly confirmed by Kautsky.'

'Kautsky rectified [Plekhanov's] mistake by pointing out that the bourgeoisie was not the driving force of the Russian revolution, that in *that* sense the days of bourgeois revolutions had passed.'

'The victory of the bourgeois revolution is impossible in our country *as the victory of the bourgeoisie.* This sounds paradoxical, but it is a fact. . . . This peculiarity does not eliminate the bourgeois character of the revolution. . . . It only determines the counter-revolutionary character of our bourgeoisie and the necessity of a dictatorship of the proletariat and the peasantry for victory *in such* a revolution. For a "coalition of the proletariat and the peasantry" [Kautsky], winning *victory* in a bourgeois revolution, happens to be nothing else than the revolutionary-democratic dictatorship of the proletariat and the peasantry.'

'Plekhanov . . . confused the "general character" of the revolution, *its social and economic content,* with the question of the motive forces of the revolution. . . . Kautsky immediately detected Comrade Plekhanov's errors and *corrected them* in his reply. As regards the social and economic content of the revolution, Kautsky did not deny its bourgeois character – on the contrary, he definitely recognised it.'[42]

---

[42] V. I. Lenin, *Collected Works* (referred to henceforth as CW), Vol. 11, pp. 372–3, 410–1; Vol. 13, p. 353; Vol. 15, pp. 56–7, 375.

Embodying as they do a view of the Russian revolution which we have called, and which Lenin himself at one point calls, paradoxical, these passages serve to focus attention on the basic community between Lenin's and Luxemburg's positions on this matter. The only differences which they bring to light, one in precision, another in emphasis, relate to the central Bolshevik formula of the period, *the revolutionary-democratic dictatorship of the proletariat and the peasantry*. In the context of what both Luxemburg and Lenin considered to be a bourgeois revolution to whose outcome the revolutionary struggle of the working class would be decisive, she was sometimes prepared, and he usually reluctant, to speak simply of *the dictatorship of the proletariat*. Given the classical connotation of the phrase, and displaying a greater concern for adopting unambiguous slogans, Lenin preferred to qualify it by the term, *democratic,* in order clearly to underline that the task of this dictatorship in Russia would be to carry out a bourgeois-democratic, and not a socialist, revolution. Secondly, it must, according to him, be a dictatorship of the proletariat *and the peasantry* because, except in alliance with the peasants, except by recognising and encouraging their revolutionary aspiration completely to destroy all the oppressive remnants of serfdom, the proletariat would be unable to consummate the bourgeois revolution in Russia. On both of the substantive points contained in these qualifications Luxemburg concurred: this has already been articulated with regard to the first of them and it must especially be emphasised now with regard to the second. For, like Trotsky, Luxemburg has sometimes been accused of overlooking the Russian peasantry and of underestimating the significance of the agrarian problem, a charge which is as absurd in her case as it is in his and which reflects the same attitude of indifference to historical and textual evidence.[43]

---

[43] Something should be said here about the contradictory nature of Lenin's own judgments regarding Trotsky's alleged oversight of the peasantry. In 1907, Lenin notes Trotsky's recognition of the 'community of interests between the proletariat and the peasantry . . . against the liberal bourgeoisie' and comments on his 'closeness' to, and 'solidarity' with, the Bolshevik view in this respect (CW, Vol. 12,

It is true that the peasantry was not as central to Luxemburg's attention as it was to Lenin's and that she did not dwell on the subject at the same length or devote the same careful study to it. But far from overlooking it, both she and Trotsky were explicit in stipulating the need for a class alliance between proletariat and peasantry. What really united them in this question was not some oversight but their common association with a slogan which differed from the Bolshevik one in laying stress on the fact of proletarian political hegemony within such an alliance. Trotsky had formulated this in July 1905: 'It goes without saying that the proletariat must fulfil its mission, just as the bourgeoisie did in its own time, with the help of the peasantry and the petty bourgeoisie. It must lead the countryside, draw it into the movement, make it vitally interested in the success of its plans. But, inevitably, the proletariat remains the leader. This is not the "dictatorship of the proletariat and the peasantry", it is *the dictatorship of the proletariat supported by the peasantry.*'[44] In 1908, this same formula was adopted in preference to the Bolshevik one

---

p. 470). In 1909, he denies that there is any such agreement (CW, Vol. 15, p. 374), and in 1915 speaks of Trotsky as having borrowed from the Mensheviks their '"repudiation" of the peasantry's role' (CW, Vol. 21, p. 419). The Stalinist way of dealing with this contradiction is simply to suppress its first term: piously to repeat Lenin's later judgments as if they were Holy Writ while ignoring the earlier one. This impeccably scientific procedure sees no obstacle in the fact that the earlier judgment is, on any scrupulous reading of Trotsky's texts, the correct one; or in the fact that between 1907 and 1915 Trotsky's views on this question did not change in any significant respect; or in the consideration that even in his later, negative judgments Lenin is unable to sustain in bald form the point that Trotsky simply repudiated the peasantry, and has to represent as either 'concession' or 'muddle' his manifest recognition of its role (CW, Vol. 15, p. 373; Vol. 21, p. 419). This is not the place to explore the reasons for these contradictory judgments on Lenin's part. Leaving aside Trotsky's 'conciliationist' stance within the party and the factional bitterness this created between himself and Lenin, we can only say in passing that Lenin's works provide no evidence that he ever read *Results and Prospects,* the text in which Trotsky gave the fullest presentation of his views. Cf. on this Trotsky, *The Permanent Revolution,* pp. 42, 75–9, 94–5; and E. H. Carr, *The Bolshevik Revolution 1917–23,* 3 vols., Harmondsworth, 1966, Vol. 1, p. 71.

[44] L. Trotsky, *1905,* London, 1972, p. 310. Emphasis added.

by the Sixth Congress of Luxemburg's own party, the Social Democracy of the Kingdom of Poland and Lithuania.[45] But, the partial junction of Luxemburg's and Trotsky's perspectives which it undoubtedly represents must be interpreted with proper care. It expressed their common assessment of the political relationship between proletariat and peasantry in Russia, and not of the relationship between bourgeois-democratic and socialist revolutions. To cite Luxemburg's association with the slogan in support of the contention that she then subscribed to the theory of permanent revolution is therefore quite wrong. It is equally wrong to see in it the proof of some major division between Trotsky and Luxemburg, on the one hand, and Lenin, on the other, over the general disposition of class forces in the Russian revolution. Where their formula emphasised the leading role of the proletariat in a proletarian-peasant alliance, Lenin's stressed only the alliance itself. Its more 'open' character, and what Trotsky was later to term the 'algebraic' aspect of Lenin's position, were due to a more sanguine estimation on his part of the independent political role that might be played, within the dictatorship projected for the completion of Russia's bourgeois revolution, by a revolutionary peasants' party.[46] Lenin was always clear however, this estimation notwithstanding, that the proletariat, under Social-Democratic leadership, must strive to remain in the forefront of the struggle: wanting to push the bourgeois revolution to the furthermost limits because its ulterior goals lay beyond them, and guided by the scientific theory of Marxism, it would be more clear-sighted and more consistently democratic than even the most revolutionary representatives of the peasantry. The mere Leninist formula, speaking only of proletariat *and* peasantry, may not have said anything about proletarian leadership. But the texts in which Lenin explained that formula did. On countless occasions, in fact, he insisted on the need for the proletariat to assume the leadership of the Russian revolu-

[45] Nettl, *op. cit.*, Vol. 2, p. 566; Frölich, *op. cit.*, pp. 94, 122.

[46] See for example CW, Vol. 8, p. 291; Vol. 9, pp. 46–7; Vol. 13, p. 121; Vol. 15, pp. 58, 374; and Trotsky, *The Permanent Revolution*, pp. 4, 65–74.

tionary movement in general and of the peasantry in particular.[47]

Lenin himself defined the extent of his differences with Luxemburg and the Polish Social-Democrats. They were limited to the 'terms' on which Social Democracy might participate, alongside the political representatives of the peasantry, in a provisional revolutionary government of the democratic dictatorship.[48] For the rest, he regarded the difference between the two slogans and the two positions as of no strategic significance. At the London Congress of 1907, he had already affirmed that the Bolsheviks and the Poles saw 'eye to eye' on the fundamental issues concerning the relationship of classes in the Russian revolution.[49] Then, in December 1908, the Poles succeeded in getting their slogan adopted at the Fifth Conference of the Russian party. When Martov tried to represent its adoption as a break with the Bolshevik position, Lenin derided him and labelled the attempt 'a model of pettifoggery': 'Is it not obvious that the same idea runs through all these formulations, that this idea is precisely the idea of the dictatorship of the proletariat *and* the peasantry, that the "formula", the proletariat *relying upon* the peasantry, *remains part and parcel* of that same dictatorship of the proletariat and the peasantry?' Both the Bolsheviks and the Poles, he went on to point out, recognised that the proletariat must play the leading role in the conquest of power and that its main ally in this would be the peasantry. 'We are at one . . . against the Mensheviks', he concluded, '*on all essentials, and . . . disagree only on minor points.*'[50]

The existence of this unanimity over essentials is confirmed by the passages from Luxemburg's and Lenin's writings adduced above. When she spoke of the pronounced proletarian character and methods of the Russian revolution, and when

[47] For a mere fraction, but representative sample of such occasions, see CW, Vol. 8, pp. 539–40; Vol. 9, pp. 72, 121, 177–8; Vol. 12, pp. 139, 458; Vol. 13, p. 115; Vol. 15, pp. 349, 379.

[48] CW, Vol. 15, pp. 373–4.

[49] CW, Vol. 12, pp. 469–70.

[50] CW, Vol. 15, pp. 368–70. Last emphasis added.

he said that the bourgeoisie had ceased to be a revolutionary class and that, in *that* sense, the days of bourgeois revolutions were over, each was registering what could be called a dislocation between the social content of the Russian revolution and the social forces alone capable of carrying it through. A bourgeois revolution in spite of or against the bourgeoisie: by this general characterisation, both of them condemned the Menshevik accommodation to liberalism as well as the expectation, supporting it, that the Russian revolution might furnish a new instance of the 'classical' Marxist model in which the bourgeoisie, universal class, represents its particular interest as general and rouses the people to an assault against absolutism. A bourgeois revolution, but made by the proletariat, leading the peasantry: to that extent at least, this revolution could not be a simple historical repetition, another edition of 1789 translated into Russian. To that extent also it foreshadowed its future, proletarian successor. The developing class antagonism between bourgeoisie and proletariat had firmly set its imprint on the very first stages of Russia's bourgeois revolution. The latter, as Luxemburg put it, already embodied a conflict which ran counter to the domination of capital.[51] More than once during 1905, Lenin made the same point.

'Like everything else in the world, the revolutionary-democratic dictatorship of the proletariat and the peasantry has a past and a future. Its past is autocracy, serfdom, monarchy and privilege. . . . Its future is the struggle against private property, the struggle of the wage-worker against the employer, the struggle for socialism. . . . Of course, in actual historical circumstances, the elements of the past become interwoven with those of the future; the two paths cross. Wage-labour with its struggle against private property exists under the autocracy as well; it arises even under serfdom. But this does not in the least prevent us from logically and historically distinguishing between the major stages of development. We all contrapose bourgeois revolution and

[51] See above text for n. 37 of this essay.

socialist revolution; we all insist on the absolute necessity of strictly distinguishing between them; however, can it be denied that in the course of history individual, particular elements of the two revolutions become interwoven?'

'Naturally, as a result of the special position which the proletariat occupies in capitalist society, the striving of the workers towards socialism, and their alliance with the Socialist Party assert themselves with elemental force at the very earliest stages of the movement. But purely socialist demands are still a matter of the future: the immediate demands of the day are the democratic demands of the workers in the political sphere, and economic demands within the framework of capitalism in the economic sphere. Even the proletariat is making the revolution, as it were, within the limits of the minimum programme and not of the maximum programme.'[52]

From the same point of departure, namely, the dislocation between social content and motive forces of the Russian bourgeois revolution, Trotsky's destination was the theory of permanent revolution. This was not based, as his detractors would have it, on ultra-leftist maximalism, a desire to 'skip' the bourgeois stage, and so forth. It was due to the conviction, unique to him and wholly correct, that the necessary *logical* distinction between the two revolutionary stages could not be transposed into a simple *chronological* succession within the real, historical process. That process, on the contrary, would so thoroughly combine with one another not just particular elements of the bourgeois and proletarian revolutions, but their decisive substantive contents – a peasant agrarian revolution with the establishment of a workers' state, the destruction of the Tsarist state apparatus with the first encroachments on capitalist property – as to confute any neat or clear-cut historical periodisation. The *organic* combination of revolutionary stages was a strategic inference on Trotsky's part from the same correlation of forces that lay at the centre of

[52] CW, Vol. 9, pp. 84–5 (and cf. pp. 307–8, 443–4); Vol. 10, p. 77.

Lenin's and Luxemburg's vision: a consequence of the extent to which capitalist relations had seized both the towns and the countryside of Russia, producing thereby, on the one side, a highly concentrated and militant proletariat, on the other, a bourgeoisie only weakly liberal where it was not downright reactionary, and between them a sharp class antagonism in a country still governed by an absolutist state and entrammelled by survivals of serfdom. The theory of permanent revolution, by which Trotsky, from 1905 onwards, linked the bourgeois to the proletarian revolution and the minimum to the maximum programme, was anchored in what he was later to designate the law of 'combined and uneven development'.[53]

Before 1917, neither Lenin nor Luxemburg was able to make this link, each remaining faithful to a conception in which the theoretical constructs, bourgeois revolution/proletarian revolution, had to find their counterparts in two discrete historical stages. That conception was confounded by the course of events during 1917, and they then crossed its limits. However, that they were able to take this step with no great difficulty is explained by the fact that both of them had already pushed the conception of separate stages *to* its very limits. Between the Mensheviks, who also subscribed to it, and themselves they dug what in real political terms was an abyss, repudiating, as we have seen, the idea of a bourgeois revolution so 'pure' that any independent proletarian struggle against the bourgeoisie should be postponed. Nor did they hesitate, in their central slogans as well as in the whole impetus of their strategic thinking, before the idea, truly scandalous to the Mensheviks, of a bourgeois revolution so 'impure' that the proletariat would have actually to wield or share political power to carry it out. This last point is the crux of the matter. The theory of stages never served Lenin and Luxemburg, in the way it did the Mensheviks, as a reason for curbing or moderating the mass struggle and revolutionary initiatives of

[53] L. Trotsky, *The History of the Russian Revolution,* 3 vols., London, 1932–3, Vol. 1, pp. 24–6.

the proletariat, or for compromising with liberalism, because the element of paradox and dislocation which they introduced into this theory went to the point of envisaging, as a proximate objective, the seizure of political power by an alliance of class forces under the leadership of revolutionary Social Democracy.[54] Furthermore, both of them were insistent that, if this power could not at once be used to embark on the transition to socialism, its most immediate achievements, in the shape of a bourgeois-democratic republic, a solution of the agrarian problem, a freer and more rapid development of capitalism, etc., would create the terrain on which the struggle for socialism *could* be begun in earnest. For that reason, Social Democracy must not for a moment compromise its political and ideological independence or water down its commitment to the full, i.e. maximum, programme but must rigorously preserve, throughout the course of the bourgeois revolution, its profile as a revolutionary *socialist* party. In doing so, it would give notice that while standing at the head of the struggle for a democratic republic, for the satisfaction of the most pressing needs of the peasantry, its perspectives did not end there.

By contrast with the Menshevik attitude, therefore, for Lenin and Luxemburg the revolutionary struggle of the Russian proletariat was not something to be put back into the indefinite future. Social Democracy had, on the contrary, to project as very *practical* goals for that struggle, first, a conquest of power for the consummation of the bourgeois revolution, then, the utilisation of this revolution's fruits, of the bourgeois-democratic political and economic conditions which it would create, to begin the struggle for socialism. From here it was not a big step to the realisation that the proletariat, if it came to power with the peasantry, would have in the very course of consummating the bourgeois revolution to take the first transitional measures towards socialism : it could not stop to leave intact the economic power

[54] See for example CW, Vol. 8, pp. 173, 285; Vol. 11, pp. 373–4, 410; Vol. 15, pp. 56–7, 349, 361–4.

of the bourgeoisie, much less countenance delivering political power into its hands, since such 'self-restraint' in a situation of acute class warfare would jeopardise even the objectives of the minimum programme by inviting a counter-revolution. It was not a big step to the realisation that, if the bourgeois revolution had to be made against the resistance and opposition of the bourgeoisie itself, then the social and class basis for a bourgeois-democratic polity was absent from the Russian social formation. Taking this step in 1917, Luxemburg and Lenin came to stand on the same ground as Trotsky. Lenin reached that destination at the Finland Station, proceeding with the *April Theses* to throw the Bolshevik party into confusion.

In the light of the above one can better understand why, despite Trotsky's greater strategic foresight in this matter, Lenin's historical contribution to the success of the October Revolution must be judged, if this kind of balance sheet can be made at all, to have been the greater one. For, during the years when Trotsky elaborated and defended the more adequate perspective, Lenin, who dismissed it, was building the political instrument for its implementation. Of course, the ability to make this judgement depends on the hindsight that Lenin proved capable not only of adjusting his own positions in time but also of overcoming the Bolshevik party's resistance to making the same adjustment. Nor was that such an automatic thing. Lenin may have made the transition with no great difficulty, but it took all of his political energy and his immense authority amongst his followers to break down their incomprehension of, and opposition to, this change of course. The point however remains that the transition was made. In that sense, the deficiency in Lenin's overall political orientation was capable of being rectified in time. The same cannot be said about the organisational weakness which resulted from Trotsky's 'conciliationism'.[55] The finest political strategy

[55] To avoid all possible misunderstanding: we speak here only of the *organisational consequence* of Trotsky's alignment in the factional struggle and not of its theoretical/political source, which *was* rectified in good time. We utterly reject the argument that Trotsky's adhesion to the Bolshevik Party in 1917 reflected no real change in

in the world is nothing but an abstraction if it is not translated into a material, organisational force in place at the right moment to implement it. Trotsky understood this even before 1917, for he was no simple spontaneist and did not, in theory, deny the importance of the revolutionary party. Nevertheless, the practical effect of his hostility, before 1917, to the Leninist party project and of his persistent and abortive efforts, in those years, to reconcile the Bolshevik and Menshevik factions, was that he entered 1917 with a perspective which, however correct, was also disembodied, having no effective political vehicle for its realisation. It is quite utopian to imagine that, had the Bolshevik party not carried out the reorientation it did, this absence could have been made good: that in the space of only a few months an organisation capable of commanding the confidence of the broadest masses could have been built. It is still more utopian to think that the Russian proletariat could have taken power without such an organisation. Drawing the lessons of his past mistakes Trotsky made his own political adjustment and joined the Bolshevik party, a step made easier for him by Lenin's reorientation. Thereafter, he himself was always the first to acknowledge Lenin's incomparable historical merit. Its substance can be expressed in another paradox: even against his own view that the proletarian revolution was *not* yet on the agenda in Russia, Lenin forged the organisational consequence of the theory that it *was*, a revolutionary proletarian party with its sights on political power.[56]

That said, the full weight of Trotsky's own historical merit must be recognised. As we have indicated, Lenin's abandonment of the theory of stages was no mere trifle. Without it, it is, at the very least, doubtful that the October Revolution could have taken place since, before his return to Russia, his

---

his political positions, that even after 1917 he never grasped the Leninist theory of the party, that to the end his thought remained uniform in this respect. On this, see N. Geras, 'Political Participation in the Revolutionary Thought of Leon Trotsky', in G. Parry (ed.), *Participation in Politics,* Manchester, 1972, pp. 151–68.

[56] Cf. D. Avenas, *Économie et politique dans la pensée de Trotsky,* Paris, 1970, pp. 26–34.

closest lieutenants in the Bolshevik party were completely impervious to the notion and possibility of an imminent proletarian revolution in Russia. Their initial response to the February Revolution was governed by the limitation of Leninism, its fidelity to the theory of stages, and this threatened momentarily to submerge the whole difference between Bolshevism and Menshevism in a common endorsement of the bourgeois, and far from revolutionary, Provisional Government. Their response thereby validated Trotsky's judgement of 1909 that, despite its considerable distance from Menshevism whose 'anti-revolutionary aspects' were already apparent, Bolshevism secreted a similar aspect which would become a danger only with the advent of revolution itself.[57] Lenin's response, however, was governed by the ability to go beyond both the limitation and the letter of his own erstwhile perspective in order to preserve its whole revolutionary spirit and impetus against such a miserable denouement. This difference in reaction was in part a product of the profound tension at the heart of the Leninist perspective, a tension which reflected its transitional status between a mechanistic theory of stages and the theory of permanent revolution. In Lenin's case, this transition was completed in 1917. But the drama of that year also confirmed that it could not be taken for granted and that the failure to make it would have the most reactionary political consequences. If further confirmation of this is needed, it exists abundantly, in the sequel of the Twentieth Century, in the politics of all those Communist Parties, Stalinist and 'de-Stalinised', which, having resurrected the theory of stages against Trotskyism and the mature post-revolutionary positions of Lenin, took the path of reformism. With a variety of names, from the Popular Front to the British Road, they covered a uniform and far from accidental confusion: of the wholly correct point that democratic demands and reforms are of vital importance to the workers' movement with the wholly incorrect point that until these have been won no real struggle for socialism can

[57] Trotsky, *1905*, pp. 316–7; cf. *The Permanent Revolution*, pp. 111–3.

be begun. By this confusion they have managed and still manage to satisfy themselves, even where it is no longer possible to talk seriously of the bourgeois revolution, that the struggle for socialism is always for tomorrow and never – God preserve them from ultra-leftism! – for today.

What, then, accounts for Lenin's and Luxemburg's failure, before 1917, to transcend the limits of the reigning Social-Democratic orthodoxy concerning stages? A partial answer, itself in need of further explanation, is that it was their tendency to equate *that* orthodoxy with one of the most central, and for them indisputable, tenets of classical Marxism: the thesis that there can be no socialism except on the basis of very highly developed productive forces and of the over-whelming predominance within social production of a modern industrial proletariat. What was at fault was the equation and not the classical tenet. The latter, on the contrary, bears repetition and reaffirmation in these days of Maoist enthu-siasm and in view of the radical impoverishment which the concept of socialism has had to suffer in order that it might accommodate realities too well-known to need rehearsal here. In its Marxist meaning, socialism requires, beyond the expropriation of capitalist property, levels of productivity which can begin to release men from the tyrannies of labour and the division of labour; the existence of a collective work-force possessing the scientific and cultural prerequisites to achieve the fullest popular control of the production process; a populace which is capable of sustaining unprecedentedly advanced forms of direct democracy. Lenin and Luxemburg understood these requirements and they therefore refused the notion that backward Russia with its vast peasantry might immediately be ripe for socialism. The insistence on the necessity of a separate bourgeois-democratic stage was, for both of them, merely the equivalent of this refusal. Although it was no part of the theory of permanent revolution to claim that Russia was immediately ripe for socialism, Trotsky did not accept this equation. The error in it, which he perceived, arose from the belief that in Russia those material precondi-tions of socialism which we have mentioned had to be achieved in more or less *the same way* as they had been achieved in the advanced capitalist countries.

It would be wrong simply to locate the source of this belief in certain formulations from the works of Marx. The latter, to be sure, had written in the preface to *Capital* that 'The country that is more developed industrially only shows, to the less developed, the image of its own future.' But he had also protested vigorously against the attempt to 'metamorphose my historical sketch of the genesis of capitalism in Western Europe into an historico-philosophic theory of the general path every people is fated to tread . . . in order that it may ultimately arrive at the form of economy which ensures, together with the greatest expansion of the productive powers of social labour, the most complete development of man'.[58] This protest was known within Russian Social Democracy for the very good reason that it had been made in connection with the historical possibilities facing Russia. As early as 1894, in fact, Lenin had rejected the allegations that Russian Marxists counted on the development of capitalism in Russia out of a commitment to some supra-historical dogma, that they thought this development to be inevitable because that was what had happened in the West. What they maintained against the Russian populists was only that Russia *had embarked,* already and irreversibly, on the course of capitalist development and that any strategic projections for the Russian revolutionary movement must be firmly situated within an analysis of that fact and its consequences.[59] All the same, the projections which Russian Social Democracy proceeded to make out of this registration of fact did, for the most part, reflect a belief that Russia, having taken the path of capitalist development, would now have to conform to one of the 'models' of historical progress which had been provided by the older capitalist nations. The vitality of this belief should

[58] K. Marx, *Capital,* 3 vols., Moscow, 1961–2, Vol. 1, pp. 8–9; K. Marx and F. Engels, *Selected Correspondence,* Moscow, n. d., p. 379.

[59] CW, Vol. 1, pp. 191–5.

not be underestimated. It had an especially strong historical root in the Russian Empire. For, Marxism took shape and grew there in a soil cultivated by the fierce polemic against populism, an ideological antagonist which fused utopian and obscurantist notions into a vision of some uniquely Russian way to socialism.

We quoted earlier from Luxemburg's text of 1903 on the Proletariat Party, bringing out her contention that bourgeois society must pass through all the 'necessary' stages of economic and political development, in particular the parliamentary stage, before any transition to socialism might be conceivable. That is one side of the picture. The other is the ideas with which she was taking issue. She was contesting, first, the idea that Russia could create an indigenous type of socialism founded on the traditional peasant commune, and could simply bypass or undo the results of a capitalist development which was deemed by the populists, insofar as they recognised it at all, to be an alien transplant in the Russian social body. She was contesting, secondly, the Blanquist confidence in the efficacy of political will-power, the illusion that socialism could be ushered in without further ado by the conspiracy and the coup, the tendency to belittle in their favour the on-going work of proletarian organisation and education and the importance of the struggle for simple, democratic demands and economic reforms. She was challenging, in short, the notion of a miraculous leap, out of Russian backwardness and across all objective obstacles, into socialism. Against the 'fantastic concept of the . . . "independent" path to socialism in Russia', she upheld the most elementary acquisitions of historical materialism: 'The ABCs of . . . Marxian socialism teach that the socialist order is not some sort of poetic ideal society, thought out in advance, which may be reached by various paths in various more or less imaginative ways. Rather, socialism is simply the historical tendency of the class struggle of the proletariat in . . . capitalist society against the class rule of the bourgeoisie. Outside of this struggle . . . socialism cannot be realised – neither through the propaganda of the most ingenious creator of a socialist utopia nor through peasant wars or revolutionary conspiracies.'[60] The same applies in Lenin's case. When Lenin, on occasions too numerous to reckon, emphasises the bourgeois-democratic character of the Russian revolution and the necessity of 'a clear line of demarcation' between minimum and maximum programmes, his target is only rarely Trotsky, whom he then convicts, and in the most cursory fashion, of being 'unclear' about the relationship between bourgeois and socialist revolutions or of 'mixing up different historical periods'.[61] Usually that emphasis is made in explicit contrast to the populist ideas against which Lenin, in the 1890s, acquired his basic theoretical and political formation. We cite just one, fairly typical passage, dating from 1905:

'Marxists are absolutely convinced of the bourgeois character of the Russian revolution. What does that mean? It means that the democratic reforms in the political system, and the social and economic reforms that have become a necessity for Russia, do not in themselves imply the undermining of capitalism, the undermining of bourgeois rule; on the contrary, they will, for the first time, really clear the ground for a wide and rapid, European, and not Asiatic, development of capitalism; they will, for the first time, make it possible for the bourgeoisie to rule as a class. The Socialist-Revolutionaries cannot grasp this idea, for they do not know the ABC of the laws of development of commodity and capitalist production; they fail to see that even the complete success of a peasant insurrection, even the redistribution of the whole of the land in favour of the peasants . . . will not destroy capitalism at all, but will, on the contrary, give an impetus to its development and hasten the class disintegration of the peasantry itself. . . . Since the rule of the bourgeoisie over the working class is inevitable under capitalism, it can well be said that a bourgeois revolution expresses the interests not so much of the proletariat as of the bourgeoisie. But it is quite

[60] 'In Memory of the Proletariat Party', Howard, pp. 201–2; and see the whole of pp. 186–93, 197–209.

[61] CW, Vol. 15, p. 371; Vol. 16, p. 379.

absurd to think that a bourgeois revolution does not at all express proletarian interests. This absurd idea boils down either to the hoary Narodnik theory that a bourgeois revolution runs counter to the interests of the proletariat, and that, therefore, we do not need bourgeois political liberty; or to anarchism which denies any participation of the proletariat in bourgeois politics, in a bourgeois revolution and in bourgeois parliamentarism. From the standpoint of theory this idea disregards the elementary propositions of Marxism concerning the inevitability of capitalist development on the basis of commodity production. Marxism teaches us that at a certain stage of its development a society which is based on commodity production and has commercial intercourse with civilised capitalist nations must inevitably take the road of capitalism. Marxism has irrevocably broken with the Narodnik and anarchist gibberish that Russia, for instance, can bypass capitalist development, escape from capitalism, or skip it in some way other than that of the class struggle, on the basis and within the framework of this same capitalism.'[62]

The foregoing attests to what was one of the most crucial ideological components in these Marxist controversies over the nature of the Russian revolution. In play here were not simply the exigencies of abstract reason. As in all such debates, the reason of the protagonists had to cut a path through the immediate, familiar, and for them very material, reality of certain specific and determinate ideological constructs. Until 1905, the suggestion that the Russian revolution might be anything other, or more, than bourgeois-democratic in its objectives was not one that was open to any number of interpretations. It stood for one thing and one thing alone: Russian populism. It thereby represented, for all its concision, a whole constellation of ideas in which the most primitive tactical concepts sat side by side with a failure to appreciate the extent to which Russia had already come within the orbit of capitalism, this incomprehension in turn sitting adjacent to the

[62] CW, Vol. 9, pp. 48–9; cf. p. 309, and Vol. 8, pp. 288, 294, 300, 384, 471.

vision of a socialism which could forgo the material and cultural achievements of capitalism and the efforts of an organised, politically conscious working class. The suggestion, in other words, came to be associated with a general assault against Marxism. In resisting that assault, Luxemburg and Lenin (and not only they) also rejected the suggestion associated with it and, by a kind of ideological reflex, they continued to do so even when, after 1905, a lone voice from within the ranks of Social Democracy itself began to maintain that the Russian revolution could be something more than a bourgeois-democratic one on the basis now of Marxist and not populist premises. Trotsky on his own could not repair, to the satisfaction of his comrades, the discredit into which this notion had fallen. Nor could he overturn their belief in the applicability of Western European models and historical stages to Russia. That belief was understandably strong for having been born and bred in opposition to a 'socialism' proud of its Russian nationality and more or less contemptuous of the products of European civilisation. Since the attribution of such a belief to Lenin is likely to be contentious, the time and trouble will here be taken to exhibit its presence in his writings.

Early in 1905 Lenin raised the following question about the Russian revolution: 'Will it go on to the *complete* overthrow of the tsarist government and the establishment of a republic? . . . Or will it limit itself to a curtailment of tsarist power, to a monarchist constitution? In other words, are we to have a revolution of the 1789 type or of the 1848 type?' It is true that he immediately went on to add an important qualification: 'We say *type* in order to dispose of the preposterous idea that there can be any repetition of the irrevocably vanished social, political, and international situations of 1789 and 1848.'[63] As has already been indicated, for Lenin a straightforward historical repetition was out of the question owing, for one thing, to the central role which would be played in the Russian revolution by a modern, industrial proletariat

[63] CW, Vol. 8, p. 257.

under the leadership of a Marxist party. Nevertheless, if 1789 and 1848 could serve him even as analogues, it was because in respect of their different political offspring they did resemble the two alternative lines of development which he foresaw for the Russian revolution. Social-Democrats must work for the first outcome, a consummated bourgeois revolution issuing in a democratic republic and political conditions most advantageous to the future struggles of the working class. But they had also to reckon with the possibility of a miscarriage, a failed bourgeois revolution ending in a compromise between the liberal bourgeoisie and the autocracy, and in constitutional concessions which would circumscribe the latter's power without destroying it. In either case the Russian workers' movement would be faced on the morrow of the revolution with political institutions familiar to the more advanced capitalist countries. To *this* extent, it would have to repeat in the early Twentieth Century some variant of the revolutionary experience which these countries had long ago lived through and left behind. Throughout 1905 Lenin continued to invoke the alternative revolutionary models of 1789 and 1848, the tradition of the dead generations impinging even on his astute brain.[64]

These projections concerning Russia's political future found their counterparts in the alternative lines of economic development which Lenin in this period envisaged. During 1905 itself he did not go beyond rather general allusions on this score: he argued, as we have seen, that the Russian revolution would, if successful, 'clear the ground for a wide and rapid, European, and not Asiatic, development of capitalism'; on another occasion he suggested in passing that, in the event of failure, 'Russia will meet the fate of Turkey –

[64] See CW, Vol. 8, pp. 291, 385; Vol. 9, pp. 58–9, 241–2, 261; and see, by contrast, Trotsky's clear rejection of these analogies on the very first page and in the whole third chapter of *Results and Prospects* (pp. 168, 184–93). Cf. also his observation of 1909: 'In contrast to the populists, our Marxists have refused to recognise Russia's "special nature" for so long that they have come, in principle, to equate Russia's political and economic development with that of Western Europe.' *1905*, p. 313; and Avenas, *op. cit.*, p. 7.

a long painful decline and disintegration'.[65] In the years following 1905, however, Lenin both replaced these vague analogues with others more precise and dwelt on the replacements at greater length. The change was inspired partly by his close attention to the agrarian problem and to the evolution in progress in the Russian countryside. In any case, he now argued that the development of capitalism in Russia would take place either along Prussian, or – by a decisive shift to the West – along American lines, these alternatives depending respectively on whether the revolution was defeated or carried to completion. In 1908 Lenin wrote:

'Either the latifundia remain, and gradually become the basis of capitalist economy on the land. This is the Prussian type of agrarian capitalism, in which the Junker is master of the situation. For whole decades there continue both his political domination and the oppression, degradation, poverty and illiteracy of the peasant. The productive forces develop very slowly. . . . Or else the revolution sweeps away the landed estates. The basis of capitalist agriculture now becomes the free farmer on *free* land, i.e., land clear of all medieval junk. This is the *American* type of agrarian capitalism, and the *most rapid development of productive forces* under conditions which are more favourable for the mass of the people than any others under capitalism. In *reality* the struggle going on in the Russian revolution is not about "socialisation" and other absurdities of the Narodniks . . . *but about* what road capitalist development of Russia will take: the "Prussian" or the "American".'

'The genuine historical question which objective historical and social development is putting to us is: a Prussian or an American type of agrarian evolution? A landlords' monarchy with the fig-leaf of a sham constitution, or a peasant (farmers') republic? . . . We cannot get rid of the "bourgeois state". Only petty-bourgeois philistines can dream of doing so. Our revolution is a bourgeois revolution precisely because the

[65] CW, Vol. 8, p. 540.

struggle going on in it is not between socialism and capitalism, but *between two forms of capitalism,* two paths of its development, two forms of bourgeois-democratic institutions.'[66]

These alternatives were, again, ones to which Lenin made repeated reference and their relationship to the two types of revolution he had in view is clear. We do not pretend that his politico-economic hypotheses in these years were obtained simply from an amalgam of such historical comparisons. To do so would be a travesty given the painstaking research devoted by him to the specificities of Russian society and apparent throughout his work. These were precisely comparisons, not substitutes for empirical analysis, and their status as such was signalled by Lenin whenever he had occasion to appeal to them. However this may be, and when full allowance has been made for the customary *mutatis mutandis,* the manner in which Lenin used, and continually returned to, these historical examples points to the conviction on his part that Russia could not avoid traversing a course similar to the ones mapped out by the advanced capitalist countries: the stages of development derived, in the traditional Marxist periodisation, from the history of those countries must be valid, by and large, for each capitalist country taken on its own. The same conviction is evident in the dichotomy he consistently set up between Europe, on the one hand, and Russia on the other, the former having already entered the epoch of proletarian revolutions and the latter not yet having done so.[67] According to Lenin it was a mistake of which Trotsky was guilty to 'mix up different historical periods and compare Russia, which is going through her bourgeois revolution, with Europe, where these revolutions were completed long ago. In Europe the real political content of Social-Democratic work is to prepare the proletariat for the struggle for power against the bourgeoisie, which already holds full sway in the state. In Russia, the question is *still only one of*

[66] CW, Vol. 15, pp. 160, 175; and cf. Vol. 3, pp. 32–3; Vol. 12, pp. 356, 465; Vol. 13, pp. 239, 343.

[67] CW, Vol. 8, pp. 298, 471; Vol. 9, p. 109; Vol. 21, pp. 418–9.

creating a modern bourgeois state, which will be similar either to a Junker monarchy . . . or to a peasant bourgeois-democratic republic'.[68] This is not to say that Lenin regarded the Russian revolution as an exclusively local affair, unfolding in its own place and in its own time without any relationship to the class struggle in Europe. On the contrary, he did situate it in its European context and did try to fathom its international implications. However, this did not alter the fundamental outlines of his conception, only the tempos of development which it envisaged. In other words, a victorious bourgeois revolution in Russia could, he held, act as a powerful stimulus to proletarian revolutions in the West. These in turn would, if successful, help to protect Russia from the danger of a restoration and to consolidate the gains of its bourgeois revolution, providing at the same time an international milieu which would facilitate the Russian proletariat's own struggle for socialism. In that event, the duration of the Russian journey could be shortened.[69] Nevertheless, what remained in the Leninist conception was the belief that Russia had to follow in the wake of Europe, to complete the bourgeois-democratic stage before embarking on the socialist, and so on. This belief in a 'necessary' historical order Lenin sustained unquestioningly right up to 1917, even his solitary reference to the prospect of uninterrupted revolution leaving it perfectly intact. We want to dwell on this last point for a moment.

The reference in question occurs in an article written during 1905: 'From the democratic revolution we shall at once, and precisely in accordance with the measure of our strength, the strength of the class-conscious and organised proletariat, begin to pass to the socialist revolution. We stand for uninterrupted revolution. We shall not stop half-way. . . . We shall bend every effort to help the entire peasantry achieve the democratic revolution, *in order thereby to make it easier* for us, the party of the proletariat, to pass on as quickly as possible

[68] CW, Vol. 16, p. 379.

[69] See CW, Vol. 8, pp. 258, 287–8, 303, 439, 535, 541–2; Vol. 9, pp. 261, 412; Vol. 10, pp. 91–2; Vol. 13, p. 327; Vol. 15, p. 180; Vol. 21, p. 420. And cf. Trotsky, *The History of the Russian Revolution,* Vol. 3, pp. 372–3.

to the new and higher task – the socialist revolution.'[70] Save for its use of the formula, 'uninterrupted revolution', the passage is in no sense an unusual one in Lenin's writings of this period. It expresses an idea which he put forward dozens of times and which was touched on earlier, the idea, namely, that the completion of the democratic revolution would create the preconditions for, and mark the beginning of, the proletariat's struggle for socialism.[71] If this struggle was not immediately on the agenda according to Lenin, he did clearly situate it in a foreseeable rather than remote future. In the above passage he chose to give this fact a particularly pronounced emphasis, using what was for him a quite uncharacteristic formulation which suggested, contrary to many of his other formulations, that the period between the two revolutions might not after all be a very extended one. That would depend on the degree of proletarian strength within the overall relation of political forces existing in the aftermath of the democratic revolution. When this passage is set beside some of the other material which has been cited, one finds in the contrast the most striking confirmation of what we have called the profound tension within the Leninist perspective: the latter continued to reproduce an orthodoxy in which the bourgeois-democratic stage was seen as a more or less lengthy period of development, and thus to circumscribe the proximate revolutionary possibilities with boundaries based on a dogmatic schema, while *at the same time* embodying a strategic approach which was revolutionary to the very core because attentive to every *real* revolutionary possibility which might present itself. Considering Lenin's thought as a whole, in its integrity and complexity, it is therefore perfectly proper to indicate, as many people have done, the important degree of continuity that there was between his perspective before 1917 and his orientation and conduct during that year. We ourselves attempted earlier to draw attention to the elements of

[70] CW, Vol. 9, p. 237.
[71] See for example CW, Vol. 8, pp. 292, 328–9, 384–5; Vol. 9, pp. 50–1, 100, 130, 136, 442–3.

that continuity. However, once that has been said, it is perfectly derisory to pretend, as the whole Stalinist tradition has done, that in 1917 Lenin made no significant break with his anterior conceptions, that these were purely and simply adequate to, and harmonious with, the subsequent course of events. This piece of hagiography is derisory for two reasons at least.

The first is that it disregards, in favour of one lonely phrase, a substantial proportion of what Lenin said and wrote during the course of twelve years. If, from 1905 onwards, he really did envisage such a running together of bourgeois-democratic and proletarian revolutions as in the event occurred; if this was his fundamental conception and not, as we contend, something which threatened from time to time to irrupt into his discourse against and despite the very different orthodoxy which resided there; how, then, could he have spoken about a development of capitalism in Russia along European, or American, lines and about the creation there of a modern bourgeois state? If Marxist concepts retain any meaning at all, these projected results of the bourgeois-democratic revolution do surely constitute something of an interruption in the revolutionary process. But the Stalinist tradition has always 'skipped over', so to speak, this aspect of Lenin's perspective. It is a tradition in fact which has failed, in fifty years, to produce so much as one account of these issues which displayed any respect for the integrity of his thought or, more generally, for the elementary requirements of serious research. The fact, in any case, remains that before 1917 Lenin spoke as if the bourgeois-democratic and proletarian revolutions were separated by precisely the kind of 'Chinese Wall' which, after 1917, he castigated Kautsky for attempting to raise between them.[72] He spoke like this repeatedly: 'any concern over too rapid a transition to the maximum programme is simply absurd'; the 'revolution will strengthen the rule of the bourgeoisie'; 'we cannot get out of the bourgeois-democratic boundaries of the Russian revolu-

[72] CW, Vol. 28, p. 300.

tion'; 'the democratic revolution will not immediately over-
step the bounds of bourgeois social and economic relationships'; 'there is not, nor can there be, any other path to
real freedom for the proletariat and the peasantry, than the
path of bourgeois freedom and bourgeois progress'; 'full
victory of the peasant uprising can only create a stronghold
for a democratic bourgeois republic'; 'what the Russian
proletariat is demanding now and immediately is not something that will undermine capitalism, but something that will
cleanse it, something that will accelerate and intensify its
development'; 'the present revolution is a *bourgeois* revolution
. . . it is proceeding on the basis of capitalist production
relations, and will inevitably result in a further development
of those same production relations . . . the rule of *capital* will
remain in the most democratic republic'; 'the aims of the
revolution that is now taking place in Russia do not exceed
the bounds of bourgeois society'; and so on.[73]

The revolution which Lenin was here talking about was to
be made, according to his own hypothesis, by workers and
peasants, who furthermore would, under the leadership of
revolutionary Social Democracy, actually conquer political
power to carry it out. One has only to remember that to
understand that the important question is not, in the end,
whether he envisaged a long or a short period of time intervening between this and the proletarian revolution. He was a
revolutionary and not a seer, took account of different possibilities. The decisive thing is *what* he envisaged intervening
between the two revolutions: and that was some period of
bourgeois political rule and capitalist economic development
conceived straight out of the history of Western Europe. But
why should a worker-peasant alliance, if it already held
effective political power, pause for any length of time to
respect the 'validity' of that model? There was no real answer
to this question other than the one already embodied in the
theory of stages. This was a necessary stage of historical

[73] CW, Vol. 8, p. 297; Vol. 9, pp. 27, 52, 57, 112, 440; Vol. 10, p. 77; Vol. 12,
pp. 333–4, 457.

development which had to be gone through before the dictatorship of the proletariat, in the strict sense, could be put on the agenda. The democratic revolution must be completed before the proletariat could 'begin to pass to the socialist revolution'. Failure to grasp this, according to Lenin, was equivalent simply to a confusion of theoretical thinking, to the blurring of an essential distinction between two different types of revolution, to anarchism, adventurism, petty-bourgeois philistinism. Until 1917 he did not, ever, entertain the possibility that the Russian masses might combine the tasks of the two revolutions, might overturn the rule of capital and *begin* the transition to socialism, even while still liquidating Russia's massive pre-capitalist past.

In 1917 Lenin not only did come to recognise that possibility but also contributed as much as any single individual could to making it an actuality of world-historical consequence. And this brings us to the second reason why the Stalinist reading of Lenin is derisory. In a first moment, and in order to accommodate the events of 1917 to the perspective he defended before then, it passes over in silence Lenin's frequent and emphatic assertion that the Russian revolution must inevitably lead to one or another type of *capitalist* development. However, because of its repugnance for the idea that Trotsky may actually have been on to something, which is more than just a matter of historical sentimentality on its part, Stalinism still wants to preserve the notion of a distinct and separate bourgeois-democratic stage. In a second moment, it therefore tries to find, in the history of the Russian revolution, something which might correspond to the clear line of demarcation between the two revolutionary stages that Lenin had previously insisted on upholding. It comes up with such a line in a simple chronology: the bourgeois-democratic and proletarian revolutions in Russia took place in February and October of 1917 respectively; Lenin's reorientation of the Bolshevik party in April, accordingly, represented no kind of departure by him from the problematic of separate stages, but was a perfectly natural response to the fact that what he had always defined as the indispensable precondition of the proletarian revolution had now been achieved. The small flaw in the argument is that this last contention is utterly false. What Lenin for an entire decade defined as the main content of the democratic stage, the tasks whose fulfilment he regarded as essential before there could be any question of going beyond the boundaries of that stage – that of sweeping away the remnants of serfdom in the Russian countryside through an agrarian revolution, and that of razing to the ground the whole apparatus of the Tsarist state – these tasks were achieved not by the February Revolution but by the October Revolution. They were achieved by, and because of the October Revolution, which means, bearing in mind Lenin's role in making that revolution possible, that they were achieved because in 1917 he ceased, finally, to regard them as *preconditions* of the proletarian revolution, understood finally that no truly thoroughgoing and consummated democratic revolution could take place in Russia except as a *consequence* of the proletarian revolution, except, that is to say, as part and parcel of a process which would initiate the transition towards socialism. The democratic revolution was not thereby 'skipped' but its tasks were inextricably combined with those of the proletarian revolution, and consequently some of the anticipated features of the democratic stage were denatured. A modern bourgeois state was not created: its rudiment, the Constituent Assembly, had a fleetingly brief life and that, furthermore, not before but after the inauguration of the proletarian dictatorship. There was no rapid development of capitalism along European lines but there was the New Economic Policy. The course of the Russian revolution did not observe any clear line of demarcation. It overturned the whole orthodox conception of a standard historical sequence valid for each country. Lenin drew the consequences of it.

'The victorious Bolshevik revolution', he wrote in 1918, 'meant the complete destruction of the monarchy and of the landlord system (which had *not* been destroyed before the October Revolution). We carried the *bourgeois* revolution *to its conclusion*.' Again: 'It was the Bolsheviks, and only the Bolsheviks, who, thanks only to the victory of the *proletarian* revolution, helped the peasants to carry the bourgeois-democratic revolution really to its conclusion.' And: 'Only the October Revolution, only the victory of the urban working class, only the Soviet government could relieve the whole of Russia, from end to end, of the ulcer of the old feudal heritage, the old feudal exploitation, landed estates and the landowners' oppression of the peasants as a whole.' In 1921: 'We solved the problems of the bourgeois-democratic revolution in passing, as a "by-product" of our main and genuinely *proletarian*-revolutionary, socialist activities ... the Kautskys, Hilferdings, Martovs ... were incapable of understanding *this* relation between the bourgeois-democratic and the proletarian-socialist revolutions. The first develops into the second. The second, in passing, solves the problems of the first.'[74]

We cannot here explore the factors which enabled Lenin to break with the orthodoxy he had defended hitherto. We will touch on only one of them, the impact of the First World War. This led first, via the debacle of European Social Democracy, to a radical reappraisal on his part of the Marxism of the Second International in which that orthodoxy, amongst others, was enshrined. Secondly, it brought out in the starkest possible way the reality and the effects of capitalism as a *global* system, setting Lenin to the study of imperialism. Out of this double reflection emerged a qualitatively different understanding of the trajectory necessary for the backward countries. The tasks assigned classically to the bourgeois-democratic revolution and the bourgeois-democratic stage, those

[74] CW, Vol. 28, pp. 301, 314, 338; Vol. 33, p. 54. There is only one way of finding any fundamental difference between this and the perspective which Trotsky elaborated out of the experience of 1905: and that is to pretend that he, by contrast with Lenin, had visualised bypassing, skipping or leaping over the democratic revolution, ignored the peasantry, even 'failed to understand the idea of the hegemony of the proletariat', and so forth. The *locus classicus* of this 'interpretation', as of the arguments treated above, is of course Stalin: see for example *Leninism, op. cit.*, pp. 22–6, 59–60, 91–3, 122–3, and *passim*. For some more recent variants, see M. Basmanov, *Contemporary Trotskyism: Its Anti-Revolutionary Nature*, Moscow, 1972, pp. 17–28; *Against Trotskyism*, Moscow, 1972, pp. 10–11; M. Johnstone, 'Trotsky: His Ideas', *Cogito* (Journal of the Young Communist League), No. 5, London, n.d. (1969?), pp. 8–16; K. Mavrakis, *Du Trotskysme*, Paris 1971, pp. 20–32. The definitive refutation of these things is contained in Trotsky's own writings.

of agrarian reform, national independence, development of the productive forces, and so on, were now clearly seen by him as part of an anti-imperialist, and therefore anti-capitalist struggle, squarely situated by him in the context of an international struggle for socialism. These countries could not simply take the path that had been trodden by the first capitalist nations, 'the path of bourgeois freedom and bourgeois progress' which Lenin in 1905 had held to be the only possible one. In 1918, he was saying by contrast: 'After the long and desperate world war, we can clearly discern the beginnings of a socialist revolution all over the world. This has become a necessity for even the more backward countries . . . irrespective of any theoretical views or socialist doctrines.'[75] Needless to say, Lenin was not denouncing theory as such, only a specific variant of it. Nor had he suddenly become a partisan of the miraculous leap into socialism, of the view that the material preconditions stipulated by classical Marxism could be evaded. Far from it. To those who, in the name of Marxism, challenged the historical legitimacy of the October Revolution, Lenin replied by asking why Russia should not 'create the fundamental requisites of civilisation in a different way from that of the West-European countries'. He still acknowledged as 'incontrovertible' the proposition that in Russia the productive forces were not sufficiently developed to make socialism possible. But the distance he had by now travelled from the orthodox inferences from that proposition can be measured in the following passage: 'You say that civilisation is necessary for the building of socialism. Very good. But why could we not first create such prerequisites of civilisation in our country as the expulsion of the landowners and the Russian capitalists, and then start moving towards socialism? Where, in what books, have you read that such variations of the customary historical order of events are impermissible or impossible? . . . It need hardly be said that a textbook written on Kautskian lines was a very useful thing in its day. But it is time, for all that, to abandon the idea that

[75] CW, Vol. 28, p. 342.

it foresaw all the forms of development of subsequent world history. It would be timely to say that those who think so are simply fools.'[76] And it would be timely, on the part of some, to recognise in all this a certain settling of accounts.

IV

'The cause of international reaction has *now*, on January 22, on the streets of Petersburg, had its bloody Jena. For on this day the Russian proletariat burst on to the political stage as a class for the first time; for the first time the only power which historically is qualified and able to cast Tsarism into the dustbin and to raise the banner of civilisation in Russia and everywhere has appeared on the scene of action.' In this manner did Rosa Luxemburg greet the beginning of the 1905 revolution. From its very first weeks she was insisting that the central driving force of the whole revolution, 'the pillar of the movement for freedom', must be the industrial working class, that only it could lead 'all the oppositional and revolutionary forces in Russian society' in a successful assault against Tsarism. 'The power and the future of the revolutionary movement', she therefore wrote, 'lies entirely and exclusively in the class-conscious Russian proletariat.'[77] However, even while emphasising this point, Luxemburg upheld the proposition that the objectives of the Russian revolution were limited to bourgeois-democratic ones.

'The Russian Revolution will, formally speaking, bring about in Russia what the February and March Revolutions [1848] brought about in Western and Central Europe half a century ago. At the same time, however – and just because it is a belated and straggling fragment of the European revolutions – it is a very special type in itself. Russia is stepping on to the revolutionary world-stage as the politically most backward country. . . . Precisely and only for this reason, contrary to

[76] CW, Vol. 33, pp. 478–80.
[77] 'The Revolution in Russia', Looker, pp. 118–20.

all the generally held views, the Russian revolution will have a more pronounced proletarian class-character than any previous revolution. It is true that the immediate objectives of the present uprising in Russia do not go beyond the limits of a bourgeois-democratic constitution, and the final result of the crisis (which may, and most probably will, last for years, alternating between flood and ebb-tide) may, if anything at all, be no more than a wretched constitution. And yet the revolution which is condemned to give birth to this political changeling will be a pure proletarian one, unlike any before it.'[78]

The development of these themes in the period that followed led Luxemburg to the strategic conclusion that the Russian proletariat should endeavour to take power in order to carry out the tasks of the bourgeois revolution. In that sense it led her, as we have argued, to the very limits of the theory of stages. But she stopped short at those limits with the idea that, for the moment, the Russian proletariat's hold on political power could be but temporary and would have to give way to a period of bourgeois-democratic rule. This conclusion was spelt out quite clearly in a short text entitled 'Blanquism and Social Democracy', which she wrote in the middle of 1906 and which, it is worth mentioning in passing, was a defence of Lenin and the Bolsheviks against the charge of Blanquism levelled by Plekhanov. The point is of interest because only two years earlier Luxemburg herself had made the same charge,[79] and the article in which she did so has served as the basis of countless attempts to freeze the differences existing between her and Lenin in 1904 into a fixed and timeless antagonism. In any case, for present purposes the main interest of the later text lies elsewhere, in its treatment of Russia's revolutionary prospects.

'If today the Bolshevik comrades speak of the dictatorship of the proletariat, they do not give it the old Blanquist

---

[78] From *Neue Zeit*, January 1905; cited in Frölich, *op cit.*, pp. 91–2.
[79] See 'Organisational Questions of Russian Social Democracy', Waters, p. 118.

meaning. . . . On the contrary, they have affirmed that the present revolution could end with the proletariat, the *whole* of the revolutionary class, laying hold of the state machine. The proletariat, as the most revolutionary element, will perhaps assume its role as the liquidator of the old order by "taking power for itself" in order to oppose the counter-revolution, and to prevent the revolution being derailed by a bourgeoisie which is reactionary in its very nature. No revolution has been consummated otherwise than by the dictatorship of a class and all the signs indicate that at the present time the proletariat can become this liquidator. Evidently, no Social-Democrat entertains the illusion that the proletariat can hold on to power: if it could, it would implement its class objectives, it would realise socialism. Its forces are insufficient for that at the present moment, for the proletariat, in the strictest sense of the word, is precisely a minority of society in the Russian Empire . . . the very idea of socialism excludes the domination of a minority. Therefore, on the day of the proletariat's political victory over Tsarism, the power which it has conquered will be taken back by the majority. To speak concretely: after the fall of Tsarism, power will pass into the hands of the most revolutionary section of society, the proletariat; for the proletariat will seize all the positions and stand guard so long as power is not in the hands legally entitled to hold it, in the hands of the new government which the Constituent Assembly, as the legislative organ elected by the whole population, is alone able to determine. Now it is self-evident that it is not the proletariat but the petty-bourgeoisie and the peasantry that constitute the majority in society, and that, consequently, in the Constituent Assembly it will not be the Social-Democrats who form the majority but the peasant and petty-bourgeois democrats. We might deplore this but we can in no way change it.'[80]

[80] R. Luxemburg, 'Blanquisme et social-démocratie', *Quatrième Internationale,* No. 2, Nouvelle Série, April 1972, pp. 54–5. Luxemburg also writes: 'We do not accept Comrade Plekhanov's reproach that [the Bolsheviks] have been the victims of Blanquist mistakes during the course of the revolution. It is possible that there

The above passage resolves the ambiguities inherent in Luxemburg's tendency simultaneously to characterise the Russian revolution as bourgeois and proletarian. It is that tendency, no doubt, which has led so many people to assimilate her perspective to Trotsky's theory of permanent revolution. But if she agreed with Trotsky on the question of the *motive forces* of the Russian revolution and in that sense described it as proletarian, her own analysis fell short of envisaging the kind of telescoping of bourgeois-democratic and socialist *objectives* which was central to his perspective and, for that reason, she described the revolution as bourgeois. This difference remained even where Luxemburg developed her argument not, as above, exclusively from the relationship of class forces in Russia, but from the international context of the Russian revolution. She did this at some length in her pamphlet on the mass strike, written in the autumn of 1906, when she attempted to draw together the lessons of the previous year and, in particular, to emphasise their significance for the European workers' movement. In this pamphlet, the parallels between her own position and Trotsky's are indeed striking, emerging most clearly in the following, central passage. It too contains the kind of 'ambiguity' we have referred to; but, read carefully, it does *not* speak of the Russian revolution going beyond the limits of bourgeois-democratic objectives.

'The Russian revolution has for its next task the abolition of absolutism and *the creation of a modern bourgeois-parliamentary constitutional state*. It is exactly the same in form as that which confronted Germany at the March Revolution, and France at the Great Revolution at the end of the Eighteenth Century. But the condition, the historical milieu, in which these formally analogous revolutions took place are funda-

---

were traces of this in the organisational project drafted by Lenin in 1902, but that is something which belongs to the past; to a distant past, for today life moves fast, at a dizzying speed. These errors have been corrected by life itself.'

mentally different from those of present-day Russia. The most decisive difference is the circumstance that between those bourgeois revolutions of the West and the present bourgeois revolution in the East, the whole cycle of capitalist development has run its course. And this development has seized not only the West European countries, but also absolutist Russia. Large-scale industry with all its consequences – modern class divisions, sharp social contrasts, modern life in large cities and the modern proletariat – has become in Russia the prevailing form, that is, in social development the decisive form of production. The remarkable, contradictory, historical situation results from this that the bourgeois revolution, in accordance with its formal tasks will, in the first place, be carried out by a modern class-conscious proletariat. . . . This contradictory situation finds expression in the fact that in this formally bourgeois revolution, the antagonism of the bourgeois society to absolutism is governed by the antagonism of the proletariat to bourgeois society, that the struggle of the proletariat is directed simultaneously and with equal energy against both absolutism and capitalist exploitation, and that the programme of the revolutionary struggle concentrates with equal emphasis on *political freedom, the winning of the eight-hour day, and a human standard of material existence for the proletariat.* . . . The mass strike is thus shown to be not a specifically Russian product, springing from absolutism, but a universal form of the proletarian class struggle resulting from the present stage of capitalist development and class relations. . . . The balancing of the account with absolutism appears a trifle in comparison with the many new accounts which the revolution itself opens up. The present revolution realises in the particular affairs of absolutist Russia the general results of international capitalist development, and appears not so much as the last successor of the old bourgeois revolutions as the forerunner of the new series of proletarian revolutions of the West. The most backward country of all, just because it has been so unpardonably late with its bourgeois revolution, *shows ways and methods of further class struggle to the proletariat of Germany and the most advanced capitalist countries.'*[81]

As is clear, for Luxemburg the Russian revolution was the forerunner of the proletarian revolutions of the West only in respect of the forms of mass struggle which it had thrown up. In case there be any remaining doubt as to what she saw as the goals of this revolution, elsewhere in the same pamphlet she spoke of the mass strike in Russia as a means of 'creating for the proletariat the conditions of the daily political struggle and especially of parliamentarism'; anticipated 'the close of the period of revolution and the erection of a bourgeois-parliamentary constitutional state'; and argued that 'in Russia the great step must first be taken from an Oriental despotism to a modern bourgeois legal order'.[82] Shortly after writing the pamphlet, she made the same point in a speech in Mannheim: 'Nothing other than a constitutional bourgeois state can be created.'[83]

In May 1907, Luxemburg was a delegate to the Fifth Congress of the Russian Social-Democratic Party in London, making several contributions to the debate which took place there. The content of these contributions differed in no significant respect from the material which has already been cited. The first of them was devoted to emphasising how much German Social Democracy had to learn from the rich experience of the Russian proletariat. The latter, she argued, while leading the struggle against absolutism in Russia, was also in the vanguard of the international working class. For, it had adopted forms of action which involved the 'direct intervention of the broadest proletarian masses' and had begun to develop tactics appropriate to a period of open revolutionary struggle. In a future period of class confrontation in Germany, the German proletariat would have to build on this experience and learn to go beyond the purely parliamentarist tactics which had dominated its political development hitherto. In

[81] 'The Mass Strike, the Political Party and the Trade Unions', Waters, pp. 201–3. Emphasis added.

[82] *ibid.*, pp. 158, 199, 205.

[83] Cited in Nettl, *op. cit.*, Vol. 1, p. 370.

the context of this argument, Luxemburg again affirmed that the Russian revolution was 'not so much the last act in the series of bourgeois revolutions of the Nineteenth Century as the forerunner of a new series of future proletarian revolutions, in which the conscious proletariat and its vanguard, Social Democracy, are destined historically to play the leading role'.[84] In the major part of her second speech, Luxemburg challenged the attitude of the Mensheviks to the bourgeois parties and attacked their belief that the Russian bourgeoisie could play a revolutionary or leading role and that the proletariat should not be so 'tactless' as to adopt tactics which might frighten the liberals into the arms of reaction. The history of Western Europe, she pointed out, showed that the bourgeoisie had long since ceased to be revolutionary, nor could anything be expected of Russian liberalism which had already demonstrated its 'despairing impotence' in the face of absolutism. The tactical recipe of the Mensheviks led to the renunciation of any independent proletarian struggle and of the goals of the revolution itself. The extent to which this revolution already expressed the maturing class contradictions of capitalism in Russia could not be artificially concealed. Social Democracy, Luxemburg said, must not hesitate to hold before the Russian working class the goal 'of achieving political power in order to carry out the tasks of the present revolution'.[85]

It is not very surprising that Trotsky, at the same Congress, should have expressed his solidarity with these positions. He opened his contribution to the debate by saying that 'The point of view which Comrade Luxemburg has been developing here on behalf of the Polish delegation is very close to the point of view which I defended and still defend. If you can set up a distinction between us, then this is more a matter of individual shades of opinion than one of political direction.'[86] And, indeed, the analysis which Luxemburg had presented

---

[84] *Pyatyi (Londonskii) S''ezd RSDRP, Aprel'-mai 1907 goda, Protokoly,* Moscow, 1963, pp. 97–104. I am grateful to Michael Waller for making translations of these speeches for me.

[85] *ibid.,* pp. 383–90.

[86] *ibid.,* p. 397.

was remarkably close to his own, in terms both of its treatment of the general configuration of class forces and of its recognition that the dynamic of revolutionary struggle could end by placing the proletariat in power. The similarity between their perspectives, moreover, was reinforced by a third speech in which Luxemburg dealt with the question of the peasantry. As the vanguard of the Russian revolutionary movement, she argued, the proletariat must attempt to bring under its influence all the popular revolutionary forces, and this meant, in the first place, the peasantry. The Mensheviks were wrong to discount it for it was an objectively revolutionary force despite the elements of inconsistency and utopianism in its demands. The peasantry might not be able to play an independent political role since it always followed the lead of other, more active classes. But 'In Russia, political leadership of, and influence over, the chaotic movement of the peasantry are now the natural historical task of the conscious proletariat.' To renounce this role of leadership, Luxemburg concluded, would be the worst form of sectarianism.[87]

It is clear, in the face of all this, that Trotsky's claim was far from being an empty one. Yet, there remains, despite it, a distinction between his own and Luxemburg's positions which is more than a mere nuance. From the possibility of a proletarian seizure of power in Russia, Trotsky *alone* drew the consequence that the Russian workers could initiate a process going beyond the limits of bourgeois society, could inaugurate *the transition to socialism*. Luxemburg did not. In her speeches at the London Congress, as elsewhere, she was perfectly clear as to what she saw as the objectives and limits of this 'proletarian' revolution in Russia. That was why she spoke, for example, of the mass strike of the Russian workers as 'a means of class struggle for winning the most elementary freedoms of the contemporary class state'.[88] That was also why she repudiated the accusation that her perspective was unduly optimistic: 'If the working class extends and strengthens its

[87] *ibid.*, pp. 432–5.
[88] *ibid.*, p. 97.

battle tactics in accordance with the ever unfolding contradictions and ever widening perspectives of the revolution,
then it may fall into very complicated and difficult positions ...
I even think that if the Russian working class turns out to be
capable of fulfilling its task, that is, if, by its actions, it brings
the course of revolutionary events to the extreme limit which
is allowed by *the objective development of social relationships,*
then almost inevitably at this boundary a big temporary defeat
awaits it.'[89] It should by now be clear what kind of defeat
Luxemburg was here referring to: the defeat of having to
relinquish political power when the utmost limits of the
bourgeois revolution in Russia had been reached.

*   *   *

We do not know through what process of reflection Luxemburg, incarcerated, ceased in 1917 to regard these limits as
impassable. Suffice it to say that while, in April of that year,
she was still writing that the revolutionary action of the
Russian proletariat would again put 'the programme of 1905
on the agenda: democratic republic, eight-hour day, expropriation of the large landed proprietors';[90] by May, she was
beginning to talk of the possibility that the Russian revolution
might be 'a first proletarian revolution of *transition,* world-
historical in significance and destined to react on the totality
of capitalist countries'.[91] When the October Revolution
occurred she still feared that the proletarian dictatorship in
Russia might go down to defeat. But, as she explained in a
letter to Luise Kautsky in November, this was because of
the lack of revolutionary support from the West and 'not
because statistics show the economic development of Russia
to be too backward, as your clever husband has worked out'.[92]
Luxemburg's critical assessment of the Bolshevik Revolution,
penned in the autumn of 1918, was framed by this changed

[89] *ibid.*, p. 436. Emphasis added.
[90] 'La révolution en Russie', R. Luxemburg, *Oeuvres II : Ecrits politiques 1917–1918*, Paris, 1969, p. 21.
[91] 'Deux messages de Pâques', *ibid.*, p. 39.
[92] R. Luxemburg, *Lettres à Karl et Luise Kautsky,* Paris, 1970, p. 130.

perspective. She began with an unambiguous rejection of 'the doctrinaire theory . . . according to which Russia, as an economically backward and predominantly agrarian land, was supposed not to be ripe for social revolution and proletarian dictatorship, [and] which regards only a *bourgeois* revolution as feasible in Russia. . . . This doctrine . . . follows from the original "Marxist" discovery that the socialist revolution is a national and, so to speak, a domestic affair in each modern country taken by itself'. She went on to stress what she saw as the essential merit of the Bolsheviks: that they 'set as the aim of this seizure of power a complete, far-reaching revolutionary programme: not the safeguarding of bourgeois democracy, but a dictatorship of the proletariat for the purpose of realising socialism. Thereby they won for themselves the imperishable historic distinction of having for the first time proclaimed the final aim of socialism as the direct programme of practical politics'. She ended on a note of sober internationalism: 'In Russia the problem could only be posed. It could not be solved in Russia.'[93] Released from an imprisoning orthodoxy, Luxemburg's thought, like that of Lenin, had converged finally with the ideas of Leon Trotsky.

[93] 'The Russian Revolution', Waters, pp. 367–8, 375, 395.

III

The Mass Strike

'The masses are the decisive factor; they are the rock upon which the final victory of the revolution is erected.'[1]

Rosa Luxemburg laid great emphasis on the spontaneity of the masses. Those who know anything about her are likely to know at least that. They are unlikely to have seen any connection between it and the fact that she was a woman. But this connection has been made. The late George Lichtheim, after drawing attention to the contrast between her revolutionary positions and the reformism of E. D. Kuskova, authoress of the 'economist' *Credo,* went on to say: 'This suggests that their shared reliance on "spontaneity" against "consciousness" may have had psychological roots. At any rate there is the fact that both were women, and that Luxemburg throughout her career gave the impression of regarding conscious control as a threat to spontaneity – a typically feminine notion.'[2] The suggestion, surprising though it may be, coheres quite well with the widespread tendency to locate the source of Luxemburg's attitude towards the masses somewhere beyond or beneath the realm of rational discourse. The consensus about this amongst serious scholars extends even into the terminology by which they characterise her. Thus, C. Wright Mills spoke of the 'labour metaphysic' as

[1] 'Order Reigns in Berlin', R. Looker (ed.), *Rosa Luxemburg : Selected Political Writings,* London 1972, p. 306.
[2] G. Lichtheim, *Marxism : An Historical and Critical Study,* London 1964, p. 337 n.

being for Rosa Luxemburg 'both a final fact and an ultimate faith'. According to E. H. Carr she had 'a fanatical but utopian, almost anarchist, faith in the masses', and according to F. L. Carsten, a 'blind faith in the masses'. Lichtheim himself identified in her politics 'a species of Syndicalist romanticism', referring also to her 'vague faith in "the masses"' and to 'her mystical doctrine of loyalty to the proletariat'.[3] The language is uniform in evoking the image of some religious zealot.

The assessment offered by these writers is not wholly negative. They concur, for example, in pointing to the moral, humanitarian and democratic aspects of Luxemburg's thought. With this there is no need to quarrel – only provided one bears in mind her explicit rejection of the idea that, while classes continue to exist, there could be a classless morality or democracy.[4] She did spend a lifetime fighting against what she once termed 'the profoundest of immoralities', namely, exploitation,[5] and fighting for the proletarian democracy which would liquidate it. A deeply humanitarian impulse is transparent throughout her work. However, to place on the positive side of any balance sheet only her uncompromising commitment to these values is to damn her with faint praise. In her orientation towards the masses there was also a broad strategic insight of the utmost realism. The importance of Rosa Luxemburg resides equally in that.

*   *   *

We can define the problem that confronted Rosa Luxemburg as a revolutionary militant inside German Social Democracy before the First World War, by reference to the distinction in the party's programme between the minimum and the

[3] C. Wright Mills, *The Marxists*, Harmondsworth 1963, p. 147; E. H. Carr, *1917: Before and After*, London 1969, p. 56; F. L. Carsten, 'Freedom and Revolution: Rosa Luxemburg', in L. Labedz (ed.), *Revisionism*, London 1962, p. 66; Lichtheim, *op. cit.*, p. 319, and *The Concept of Ideology and Other Essays*, New York 1967, pp. 201–2.

[4] See 'Social Reform or Revolution', M.-A. Waters (ed.), *Rosa Luxemburg Speaks*, New York 1970, pp. 85–6.

[5] 'The Russian Revolution', *ibid.*, p. 392.

maximum demands: on the one hand, a set of demands responding to the immediate, everyday concerns of the masses and which could be realised within the framework of capitalist society; on the other hand, ultimate socialist objectives. What was, and what should be, the effective relation between these two sections of the Erfurt programme? What were the strategic and tactical implications of the distinction between them? At a very general level, Luxemburg gave the only answer possible for a revolutionary. Social Democracy had to keep a firm hold on both ends of the chain. Only by a fusion of the programme of revolutionary socialism with the daily struggle of the masses could socialism be achieved. Only if the ultimate objective was related to, and eventually made a part of, their immediate concerns could the revolution triumph. For a serious revolutionary organisation there could therefore be no question of having to choose between exclusive concentration on limited struggles and demands, and the unilateral insistence on final goals. As Luxemburg herself put it: 'The world-historical advance of the proletariat to its victory is a process whose particularity lies in the fact that here, for the first time in history, the masses of the people themselves, against all ruling classes, are expressing their will. But this will can only be realised outside of and beyond the present society. On the other hand, this will can only develop in the daily struggle with the established order, thus, only within its framework. The unification of the great mass of the people with a goal that goes beyond the whole established order, of the daily struggle with the revolutionary overthrow – this is the dialectical contradiction of the Social-Democratic movement which must develop consistently between two obstacles: the loss of its mass character and the abandonment of its goal, becoming a sect and becoming a bourgeois reformist movement.'[6]

Evidently, to stress the necessity and the difficulty of

[6] 'Organisational Questions of Russian Social Democracy', D. Howard (ed.), *Selected Political Writings of Rosa Luxemburg*, New York and London 1971, p. 304; and cf. an almost identical passage in 'Social Reform or Revolution', Waters, pp. 88–9.

steering a course between sectarian and reformist dangers cannot by itself answer any concrete question of tactics or political perspective. But even in its generality that response served a purpose in Luxemburg's earliest interventions in the political life of the German party. By it she sought to identify and to challenge Bernstein's revisionism. The controversy which broke around this as she arrived in Germany in 1898 immediately put the whole issue of the relationship between minimum and maximum programmes on the agenda. Perceiving that with his renunciation of proletarian revolution and dictatorship in favour of gradual reforms, Bernstein was choosing 'not . . . a more tranquil, calmer and slower road to the *same* goal, but a *different* goal . . . not the realisation of *socialism,* but the reform of *capitalism*',[7] Luxemburg reasserted the validity and the revolutionary essence of Social Democracy's ultimate objectives. Within this reassertion, however, there was initially an important lacuna.

We can isolate it by a closer scrutiny of the relationship postulated, in her contributions to the revisionist debate, between the struggle for reforms and the revolutionary socialist goal. Affirming of the latter that it was 'the only decisive factor distinguishing the Social-Democratic movement from bourgeois democracy and from bourgeois radicalism',[8] Luxemburg insisted that it should not be lost sight of for a moment. It must, so to speak, *inform* all the partial and limited struggles. The revolutionary goal, as she herself expressed it, must be 'harmonised' with and 'embodied' in Social Democracy's practical day-to-day activity; it should be 'inseparable' from the trade-union struggle, the struggle for social reforms and for democratic rights; it was the 'spirit' and the 'soul' of these practical struggles without which they could not in themselves be considered part of the class struggle for socialism.[9] In such terms Luxemburg tried to emphasise

[7] 'Social Reform or Revolution', Waters, p. 78.

[8] *ibid.*, p. 36.

[9] 'Opportunism and the Art of the Possible', Looker, pp. 73–4; 'Social Reform or Revolution', Waters, p. 59; 'Speeches to the Stuttgart Congress (1898)', Howard, pp. 38–9, 43.

the need for there to be some real link between the everyday fight for minimum demands and the revolutionary conquest of power: otherwise the first would become for all practical purposes an end in itself and the second 'be entirely cut off from reality', a mere slogan. One of her constant complaints against the revisionist 'practical politicians' was precisely that for them Social Democracy's programmatic demands were 'just so much baggage to be dragged around and religiously referred to so long as they have no practical significance'.[10] The inadequacy within Luxemburg's position at this time can be formulated as follows: knowing that, in an objective sense, the struggle for reforms was *not* linked by an unbroken chain to the revolutionary goal, all she could find at this stage with which to forge the missing links was the reaffirmation of the goal itself, the expression of a subjective intention. Less metaphorically: knowing full well that the struggle for reforms could not by itself *effect* the socialist goal, she confined herself to insisting that it must *express* the socialist goal. More concretely: understanding intuitively the limitation of a rigid distinction between minimum and maximum demands, Luxemburg proposed the will to overcome it but not yet a strategy or tactic.

When, in the course of her polemic against Bernstein, she writes: '*It is not true that socialism will arise automatically from the daily struggle of the working class*',[11] she thereby sums up the most central element of her argument. She categorically rejected the idea that the objectives of socialism could be dissolved into a series of partial reforms, be secured increment by gradual increment through the trade-union, electoral and parliamentary activity of the working class.[12] Nor did she see in such activity any automatic or spontaneous dynamic leading the working class towards the revolutionary conquest of power. In a general way, she did of course regard

[10] 'Speech to the Hanover Congress (1899)', Howard, p. 51; 'A Question of Tactics', *Permanent Revolution* (Journal of Workers' Fight), No. 1, Spring 1973, p. 36.
[11] 'Social Reform or Revolution', Waters, p. 59.
[12] *ibid.*, pp. 48ff, 71–2, 77; and 'Militia and Militarism', Howard, p. 144.

these activities as indispensable, for they enabled the working class to build up its political and economic strength and played an important organising and educating role. Nevertheless, Luxemburg's whole emphasis against revisionism was that, in themselves, as a self-contained tactic, they could not result in a proletarian conquest of power. On the contrary, they could be entirely detached from this latter objective in which case they would constitute the activities of a bourgeois rather than socialist party. The question of the conquest of power, of the dictatorship of the proletariat, had therefore to be posed independently, for and of itself, rather than being assumed to be the organic product of the daily struggle for minimum demands and reforms.

In a sense, Luxemburg both did and did not draw this last conclusion during the revisionist debate. By constantly emphasising the totality of Social Democracy's programmatic demands and the need to keep in view its ultimate goal, she did. This is the inner meaning of the argument that the ultimate goal should somehow inform or pervade the daily struggle. At the same time she did not because, knowing that the 'good old', parliamentary and trade-union tactic could not by itself produce the dictatorship of the proletariat, she proposed no concrete alternative strategy which could. It would be better perhaps to say that, while she understood the need to pose, as a separate question, the question of the conquest of power, she was not yet *in a position* to answer it with specific strategic proposals. In any case, it should be evident that a tactic of reforms which cannot lead to socialism is not, even when infused by or coupled with a socialist purpose, the same as a revolutionary strategy which can. That is why Bernstein's quarrel with the German party could take the form it did. He called upon it 'to emancipate itself from a *phraseology* which is actually outworn and . . . make up its mind to appear what it is *in reality* today: a democratic, socialistic party of reform'.[13] Going further with this line of reasoning Bernstein's friend, Ignaz Auer, came to the oppo-

---

[13] E. Bernstein, *Evolutionary Socialism,* New York 1961, p. 197. Emphasis added.

site conclusion: if the reality of the party was its reformist tactic and the revolutionary goals mere phraseology, then an explicit renunciation of revolutionary goals was not all that important. 'My dear Ede,' he wrote to Bernstein, 'one doesn't formally decide to do what you ask, one doesn't say it, one *does* it.'[14] These sentiments, as well as the real subsequent destiny of Social Democracy, indicate the dangers inherent in the dualism of minimum and maximum programmes. The objectives embodied in the maximum programme too easily become quite bare of practical import. They can be left to take care of themselves because they belong in an unspecified future or nowhere at all. The effective activity, the real tactic, these are tailored only to winning the minimal demands. As early as the revisionist debate Luxemburg was trying to build a bridge across that distinction in the Erfurt programme. The manner in which she did so was, for the moment, inadequate: a combination of tactical concepts she knew to be limited with an abstract emphasis on the need for a proletarian conquest of power. In 1905 the Russian masses helped put her in a position to reduce that abstraction.

Even before then, in the early years of the century, a significant change of emphasis had begun to appear in Luxemburg's writings. In connection with the Belgian general strike of 1902, and afterwards, she began to move beyond the concentration on fundamental questions of programme and to stress also the importance of 'independent mass action', of 'direct action', of finding ways 'to make the working masses increasingly aware of their own power'.[15] However, it was only the revolution of 1905 that crystallised this tendency in her thinking into the distinctive strategic concept which her name brings to mind, the concept of the mass strike. After 1905 she spoke of the mass strike as *'the method of motion of the proletarian mass,* the phenomenal form of the proletarian struggle in the revolution . . . the rallying idea of a whole period

[14] Cited in J. Joll, *The Second International 1889–1914,* London 1968, p. 94.
[15] 'At Sea', *Permanent Revolution,* No. 1, p. 43; 'Social Democracy and Parliamentarianism', Looker, p. 114.

of the class struggle lasting for years, perhaps for decades'.[16] She could speak of it in this way because the notion covered for her not the planned and orderly demonstrative action undertaken for strictly defined and limited objectives, but the very content of a revolutionary or pre-revolutionary period, the type of experience precisely that Russia had witnessed during 1905: huge strikes and demonstrations, meetings and marches, mass actions of all kinds and for a multitude of interrelated demands, and flowing backwards and forwards within a veritable tidal wave of revolt. Understood in this sense, the mass strike was not something that could be summoned forth or conjured up at will by a revolutionary political leadership, a fact which Rosa Luxemburg repeatedly emphasised. It is partly for having done so, no doubt, that she has so frequently been regarded as a spontaneist. But the charge, if it rests on this, rests either on a misunderstanding of what she meant by the mass strike or on the illusion that revolutionary situations can be commanded at will. Luxemburg knew that they cannot, that they result from objective, underground and molecular changes, and she accordingly dismissed that illusion as no more than a 'police' conception of revolution.[17] So, incidentally, did Lenin who has never, to the best of our knowledge, been taken for a spontaneist. The classical Leninist definition of a revolutionary situation identifies it as the consequence of 'objective changes . . . independent of the will not only of individual groups and parties but even of individual classes'.[18]

The strategic and tactical implications of Luxemburg's mass strike concept were, for all that, considerable. Taking cognisance of the realities of a revolutionary period, she called upon Social Democracy to begin to prepare the masses for them. It could not actually summon the revolution to appear. But nor should it now be satisfied with the old routines. It had to identify such tendencies in the present situation as would, or could, lead to struggles of mass proportions, to explain and

---

[16] 'The Mass Strike, the Political Party and the Trade Unions', Waters, p. 182.
[17] *ibid.*, pp. 160–1, 187–8.
[18] See V. I. Lenin, *Collected Works,* Vol. 21, pp. 213–4.

clarify these tendencies for the working class, to agitate for and initiate forms of mass action, and where these were beginning to emerge – as, for example, in 1910 in a campaign over the Prussian suffrage laws – to try to intensify and develop them by providing the appropriate slogans and direction.[19] It had in short to adopt an offensive strategy and one involving *mass* struggles. Canvassing such a strategy in the years before the outbreak of war, against the trade-union bureaucracy, against the party leadership, against Kautsky, Luxemburg tried to shift German Social Democracy beyond its purely electoralist and trade-unionist orientation. She tried to take the conquest of power for socialism out of the realms of propaganda and to place it on some actual agenda. She tried again to transcend the dualism of minimum demands and final goal.[20] Although she still did so upon the conceptual terrain of the Erfurt programme, the bridge in this case was of much more solid material.

It was built now out of Luxemburg's deeper understanding of the dynamics of a real revolutionary process. What she grasped particularly clearly was that it is only *through* such a process, in the actual course of it, that the masses can be won for socialism. They cannot be won by propaganda only, nor by the routine defence of their day-to-day interests within the framework of capitalism, for all that both types of activity are indispensable. By such means individuals can be won, even a sizeable revolutionary vanguard assembled. But it is a mistake to imagine that, by simple extrapolation of this accumulative process, the *masses,* in their millions, can be committed to the struggle for socialist revolution. The implantation of a revolutionary consciousness in the widest masses requires as its absolute precondition the participation of these masses in struggles of a scope and combativity which

[19] 'The Mass Strike, the Political Party and the Trade Unions', Waters, pp. 200, 205; 'The Two Methods of Trade-Union Policy' and 'The Next Step', Looker, pp. 147, 152–4.

[20] Cf. on this M. Lowy, *La théorie de la révolution chez le jeune Marx,* Paris 1970, pp. 193–4, and E. Mandel 'Rosa et la social-démocratie allemande', *Quatrième Internationale,* No. 48, March 1971, p. 18. The argument of this essay owes a great deal, in one way and another, to these two authors.

are extraordinary. The masses learn in action; as Luxemburg put it, not 'by pamphlets and leaflets, but only by the living political school, by the fight and in the fight, in the continuous course of the revolution'.[21] Because she grasped this, she had no hesitation in celebrating the spontaneous, elemental aspect of revolution – actions erupting unexpectedly, mass mobilisations not fully under the control of any leadership, struggles initiated in the hidden depths of the mass movement – the same aspect which Lenin recognised when he spoke of 'festivals of the oppressed and the exploited'.[22] She was thereby only highlighting the fact that what appears in the reformist bureaucrat's nightmare as the face of disorder, provocation or adventurism, is actually the authentic face of proletarian revolution, or at least one of its ineradicable features. The very chances of victory depend upon the bursting into political life and activity of layer after layer of previously non-politicised or unorganised workers, and to want this neatly wrapped and packaged, without spontaneous outbursts, of anger or creative initiative, is the sorriest of illusions. According to Luxemburg: 'Every real, great class struggle must rest upon the support and cooperation of the widest masses, and a strategy of class struggle which does not reckon with this cooperation, which is based upon the idea of the finely stage-managed march out of the small, well-trained part of the proletariat is foredoomed to be a miserable fiasco. . . . In the case of the enlightened German worker the class consciousness implanted by the Social-Democrats is *theoretical and latent.* . . . In the revolution when the masses themselves appear upon the political battlefield this class consciousness becomes *practical and active.* A year of revolution has therefore given the Russian proletariat that "training" which thirty years of parliamentary and trade-union struggle cannot artificially give to the German proletariat.'[23]

A related and crucial point of which Luxemburg had a lucid perception was that, in a period of mass struggles, a

[21] 'The Mass Strike, the Political Party and the Trade Unions', Waters, p. 172.
[22] *Collected Works,* Vol. 9, p. 113.
[23] 'The Mass Strike, the Political Party and the Trade Unions', Waters, pp. 198–9.

tendency exists for each serious mass action to overflow its original objectives and to generate or merge with other demands and other struggles. By virtue of this tendency, the boundary placed by bourgeois society between the economic or trade-union struggle on the one hand, and politics on the other, begins to dissolve. The strike becomes a political weapon. Political and economic demands run into one another. Partial conflicts are more frequently and more easily generalised. A dynamic takes shape which contains the *potentiality* that partial demands, immediate concerns, urgent needs, can be linked up into a global revolutionary challenge to the existing order.[24] It is evident, in the light of this perception, why Luxemburg should have argued for an extension of the Prussian suffrage agitation in 1910 by use of the political mass strike, and for an attempt simultaneously to feed into it some of the economic struggles currently in progress.[25] Evident, more generally, is the whole sense of her projected strategy as an effort to prepare, via the development of existing mass struggles over limited demands, a situation in which the question of transition to socialism could concretely be posed. Approaching the same thing from another angle, one can show that there is embodied in Luxemburg's thought here, albeit only in embryonic form, a concept of dual power.

This can be shown in both a negative and a positive way. Negatively, there is a clarity in her writing concerning the fact that parliamentary democracy is 'a specific form of the bourgeois class state'[26] and not the instrument of proletarian rule, a clarity which distances her not only from the frankly interclass political conceptions espoused by Bernstein but also from the ambiguities of Kautsky. Kautsky of course knew that the state is an organ of class rule, was for the conquest of power and the dictatorship of the proletariat. He was more than ready to counterpose the necessity of 'a decisive battle', of 'great struggles', to the proposals of

[24] *ibid.*, pp. 180–1, 184–7, 202.
[25] 'The Next Step', Looker, p. 155.
[26] 'Social Reform or Revolution', Waters, p. 56.

revisionist gradualism.[27] But from the Erfurt programme to the eve of war, he contrived to give to these 'orthodox' notions a content which was utterly anodyne and which can be read in a hundred formulas scattered through his work: about increasing the power of parliament and parliamentarism changing its character, about 'the transformation of the relation of powers in the government', about 'conquest of the state power by winning a majority in parliament and by making parliament the controller of the government'.[28] Luxemburg by contrast, even when still united with Kautsky in a common opposition to revisionism, spoke an altogether different language. According to this, parliamentarism was 'a particular social form expressing the political violence of the bourgeoisie' and Social Democracy could come to power 'only on the ruins of [the] bourgeois state';[29] Bernstein was chastised precisely for considering 'the poultry-yard of bourgeois parliamentarism as the organ by means of which we are to realise the most formidable social transformation of history, *the passage from capitalist society to socialism*'.[30] Without yet spelling out the substance of the novelty involved, these lines already testify to the awareness on Luxemburg's part that the proletarian revolution must call into being a radically new type of political power.

It is in her notion of the mass strike that the positive substance of this power begins to be elaborated. Method of motion and phenomenal form of the proletariat's revolutionary struggle, the mass strike was in her eyes a way of breaking through the barriers erected by the bourgeois state against any direct expression of the will of the masses. It was a way of releasing and galvanising their energies, of overcoming the divisions and the weakness, created by bourgeois ideology and partly by the proletarian condition itself, in order thereby

[27] See K. Kautsky, *The Road to Power,* Chicago 1909, pp. 10–12, 27–30.

[28] K. Kautsky, *The Class Struggle,* New York 1971, p. 188, and *The Road to Power,* p. 47; C. E. Schorske, *German Social Democracy 1905–1917,* New York 1970, p. 247.

[29] Cited in P. Frölich, *Rosa Luxemburg,* London 1972, pp. 69, 64.

[30] 'Social Reform or Revolution', Waters, p. 81.

both to concentrate their strength and to impart to them a sense of it. The workers, she said, 'must . . . be assembled as a mass . . . must come out of factory and workshop, mine and foundry, must overcome . . . the decay to which they are condemned under the daily yoke of capitalism'.[31] Socialism requiring by its very nature the control of the working masses over the entirety of the social process, it was not possible to envisage that the road to socialism might bypass the direct intervention and active participation of these masses in movements of an unprecedented scope and vigour. There could be no short cuts, neither putschist nor bureaucratic/administrative ones. The masses themselves must step forward, work out their own emancipation through their own efforts and experiences, have the opportunity to formulate their needs and demands in the most direct, most democratic possible way.[32] The proletarian revolution had its own specific forms proper to its unique objectives, and these it must oppose to the institutionalised power of the bourgeoisie. Luxemburg detected such forms in the process of mass struggle itself. As she wrote in 1906: 'In the peaceful "normal" course of bourgeois society . . . the political struggle is not directed by the masses themselves in a direct action, but in correspondence with the form of the bourgeois state, in a representative fashion. . . . As soon as a period of revolutionary struggles commences, that is, as soon as the masses appear upon the scene of conflict . . . the indirect parliamentary form of the political struggle ceases.'[33] Adumbrated in the mass strike she saw the forms of proletarian democracy which were required to overthrow the bourgeois state. In that sense one can say that the mass strike concept is Rosa Luxemburg's *State and Revolution;* it is dual power *avant la lettre.* Of course, relative to 1917 and the real *State and Revolution,* it is only that in embryo – we repeat this to avoid misunderstanding. In particular, Luxemburg spoke about the direct and democratic manifestation of workers' power only in the

---

[31] 'The Mass Strike, the Political Party and the Trade Unions', Waters, p. 202.

[32] See, for example, 'The Idea of May Day on the March', Howard, pp. 319–20.

[33] 'The Mass Strike, the Political Party and the Trade Unions', Waters, pp. 207–8.

process of revolutionary mass *actions ;* she did not yet speak of the nature and importance of the *organs* of proletarian democracy in which this power takes an institutionalised shape, organs which are crucial to the successful consummation of a revolutionary upheaval. However, the relevant comparison is not Lenin in 1917. It is Kautsky, Lenin and the whole of European Marxism before the First World War. Relative to this, Luxemburg was the very *first* to draw the lessons of 1905 for the advanced capitalist countries and to begin to pose the question of power there in a serious, and no longer purely propagandist way. She was the first to challenge the facile optimism of peaceful linear growth implicit in the tactics of German Social Democracy, the first to counterpose to them a Marxist strategy recognising that the power of the bourgeoisie can only be destroyed by the widest and deepest mobilisation of the masses.

In this recognition there was, to be sure, a certain confidence, or 'faith', in the masses. We shall argue in a moment that those who allege it to have been boundless are wrong to do so. Here, it will be opportune to point out that Luxemburg's lifelong emphasis on the importance of proletarian, socialist democracy was not just a matter of some praiseworthy moral commitment on her part. It was that, but not just that. For it was also a matter of the most hard-headed strategic realism. Arrayed against the proletariat in an advanced capitalist society are powers of an immense weight and density, economic, political and ideological powers which in their unity constitute the rule of the bourgeoisie. This power of capital is reproduced in a million ways, daily and hourly, in the automatic, spontaneous and not so spontaneous regularities of the social process. It is reproduced by the impersonal mechanisms of the market and the opacity of its forms, by the ideological output pouring forth from countless public and private channels, by the forces and the frauds of the bourgeois state. It can be seriously called into question *only* by organising and concentrating the numbers, the resources, the capacities which the proletariat has potentially at its command and by unleashing these in the most energetic fashion from their normal subordination to the interests of profit. Obviously this cannot be done behind the backs of the masses or on their behalf. It requires genuine organs of proletarian democracy, such as workers' councils, and the unfolding class struggles, the mass actions, which are their indispensable precondition. Such organs and such actions do not immediately dissipate the power of the bourgeoisie. But they severely dislocate and weaken it, and they begin simultaneously to pose in a material way an alternative form of rule. Stimulating and organising the capacities of the masses, they undermine the social routines sustaining bourgeois power and prepare its destruction. That is why the capitalist class cannot tolerate for any length of time a situation of mass struggles in which the institutions of workers' democracy are developing or have emerged. It will make every type of concession which is recuperable, use all the means at its disposal to head the movement off and contain it, and make ready for the contingency of a life-and-death fight. Luxemburg's mass strike orientation represented the beginnings of a theorisation of these revolutionary realities. Subsequently, during the German revolution of 1918–19, she formulated them again as follows: 'The "civil war" which some have anxiously tried to banish from the revolution cannot be dispelled. For civil war is only another name for class struggle, and the notion of implementing socialism without a class struggle, by means of a majority parliamentary decision, is a ridiculous petit-bourgeois illusion.' 'Socialism will not be and cannot be inaugurated by decrees; it cannot be established by any government, however admirably socialistic. Socialism must be created by the masses, must be made by every proletarian.'[34]

It should be added, to round out this point, that there was in Luxemburg's thinking no trace of anarcho-syndicalism nor any attitude of abstentionism towards the political institutions of bourgeois society. She tried to widen Social Democracy's horizons beyond 'the perspective of the ballot-

[34] 'The National Assembly', Looker, pp. 263–4; 'Speech to the Founding Convention of the German Communist Party', Waters, p. 419.

box'[35] and to integrate within them the dimension of direct mass action. This much is true. But she did not underestimate the importance of parliament as an arena of intervention and a platform of agitation.[36] Even in the midst of the German revolution itself, she proposed using the elections to and the floor of the National Assembly, 'counter-revolutionary stronghold erected against the revolutionary proletariat', for the purpose of mobilising the masses to sweep it away and to place power in the hands of the workers' and soldiers' councils.[37]

Earlier, we tried to show that the charges of spontaneism and economism so frequently levelled at her can find no vindication in Luxemburg's theory of capitalist breakdown.[38] The same applies with regard to her thinking on the mass strike. Correctly understood, the political and tactical conceptions at the heart of it lead away from spontaneism and economism. This is not to take back what has already been said on the question of spontaneity, namely, that in speaking about the genesis and unfolding of a period of revolutionary mass struggles, she placed due weight upon factors which are, from the point of view of the revolutionary organisation, spontaneous or objective. If she had not done that she would not have been a Marxist. But the fundamental meaning of the mass strike strategy was that the revolutionary organisation, Social Democracy putatively, must begin to prepare the so-called subjective factors. This it could not do except by breaking with the assumption that socialist class consciousness is automatically enhanced and socialism itself automatically brought nearer simply through the consistent pursuit of trade-unionist objectives and electoral success. In Luxemburg's conception, Social Democracy had to insert into its *real* perspectives the 'final' programmatic goal of the revolu-

[35] 'Concerning Morocco', Looker, p. 167.

[36] See, for example, 'Social Democracy and Parliamentarianism' and 'What Now?', Looker, pp. 114-6, 174-8.

[37] 'The Elections to the National Assembly', Looker, pp. 287-90; 'Speech to the Founding Convention of the German Communist Party', Waters, p. 421.

[38] See above pp. 13-42.

tionary conquest of power; to carry these perspectives into the class struggle and to try to link them there to the daily needs and concerns of the masses; above all, to develop forms of struggle which could conceivably lead from these immediate concerns to the conquest of power and which, towards that end, would educate the working class in the spirit of mass action. We have suggested the presence in her thought of an embryonic concept of dual power. The conclusion of all the foregoing argument is that it contains also a germ of the ideas first formulated by the Communist International in conscious opposition to the economism of its predecessor and embodied subsequently by Trotsky in the concept of the *transitional programme*. The 'Theses on Tactics' adopted, in Lenin's day, by the Third Congress of the Comintern expressed these ideas as follows: 'In place of the minimum programme of the reformists and centrists, the Communist International puts the struggle for the concrete needs of the proletariat, for *a system of demands which in their totality disintegrate the power of the bourgeoisie,* organise the proletariat, represent stages in the struggle for the proletarian dictatorship, and each of which expresses in itself the need of the broadest masses, even if the masses themselves are not yet consciously in favour of the proletarian dictatorship.'[39] Trotsky, similarly, without for a minute forswearing the defence of even 'the most modest material interests or democratic rights of the working class', insisted on the need to transcend the dualism of minimum and maximum demands by constructing the revolutionary programme around 'a system of *transitional demands,* stemming from today's conditions and from today's consciousness of wide layers of the working class and unalterably leading to one final conclusion: the conquest of power by the proletariat'.[40]

It goes without saying that the qualification which was made concerning the claim about dual power applies with

[39] J. Degras (ed.), *The Communist International 1919–1943,* Documents, Vol. 1, London 1956, p. 249. Emphasis added.

[40] L. Trotsky, *The Transitional Program for Socialist Revolution,* New York 1973, pp. 77, 75.

equal force here. Rosa Luxemburg did not actually elaborate a strategy of transitional demands: the sliding scale of wages and hours, workers' control, the workers' government, and so on. Nor is this just a detail. For if, as she correctly observed, the masses learn in action, it is important that when a period of mass action does begin to unfold, rendering them more open to revolutionary ideas, there should already exist a significant layer of worker militants familiar with a programme of such demands and capable of explaining and popularising them. Otherwise, the movement will be more easily diverted and contained by means of concessions which are recuperable. Here again, however, it is a matter of drawing attention to the *direction* Luxemburg's thought began to take before that of any of her contemporaries. Moreover, within the limits of the Erfurt programme against which she instinctively pressed, she did not, for all her emphasis on the educative effects of mass struggle, neglect the importance of prior agitation and propaganda around the totality of demands in the programme. From the revisionist debate onwards she stressed it. It was, in any case, in the revolutionary aftermath of the First World War that she broke explicitly with the problematic of the Erfurt programme. 'The Russian revolution', she wrote, '[has] inscribed the problem of socialist revolution on the agenda of history. . . . Thanks to it, socialism has emerged from the inoffensive electioneering phraseology which treats of a nebulous future and has become the crucial problem of the day.'[41] More clearly still, and with a force due to the fact that it was uttered in the midst of the German revolution, Luxemburg said at the founding congress of the German Communist Party: 'We know nothing of minimum and maximal programmes; we know only one thing, socialism; this is the minimum we are going to secure.'[42]

It should be remembered, finally, that Luxemburg waged a long political battle against a trade-union and party leader-

[41] 'Fragment sur la guerre, la question nationale et la révolution', R. Luxemburg, *Oeuvres II : Ecrits politiques 1917–1918,* Paris 1969, pp. 96–7.

[42] 'Speech to the Founding Convention of the German Communist Party', Waters, p. 413.

ship that was thoroughly bureaucratic and reformist. In this context she sometimes counterposed 'masses' to 'leaders', and there are passages where she suggested that should the leaders try to stand in the way of a revolutionary upsurge, the latter would escape their control and sweep them aside.[43] To abstract this from its polemical context, however, and conclude that mass spontaneity was for her a self-sufficient force and the nature of the leadership a matter of no consequence, is illegitimate. Even in her response to the events of 1905, where the creativity of that force was at the very centre of her attention, there are a dozen, and more, occasions on which she emphasised how much the revolution owed to the 'untiring underground work of enlightenment performed by Russian Social Democracy' in the preceding years, and how much the course of events itself was influenced by Social-Democratic agitation and direction.[44] Luxemburg's 'faith' in the masses, when all is said and done, was circumscribed by clearly defined limits. It is not just that she stated in a general way the importance of determined revolutionary leadership. She stated in a specific and precise way the consequences of its absence, to wit, the demoralisation and confusion which begin to overtake the masses in struggle when they are shown no clear way forward, and the dissipation and dispersion of all their expended energy. In lines like the following she displayed a keen perception of the real dynamics of a revolutionary situation and thereby also of the bounds of spontaneity: 'A consistent, resolute, progressive tactic on the part of the Social-Democrats produces in the masses a feeling of security, self-confidence and desire for struggle; a vacillating weak tactic, based on an underestimation of the proletariat, has a crippling and confusing effect upon the masses.' 'The expressions of the masses' will in the political struggle cannot be held at one and the same level artificially or for any length of time, nor can they be encapsulated in one and the same form.

[43] See, for example, 'The Mass Strike, the Political Party and the Trade Unions', Waters, p. 207.

[44] *ibid.*, pp. 157, 165, 169–70, 173, and 'The Revolution in Russia', Looker, pp. 119–20.

They must be intensified, concentrated and must take on new and more effective forms. Once unleashed, the mass action must go forward. And if at the acknowledged moment the leading party lacks the resolve to provide the masses with the necessary watchwords, then they are inevitably overcome by a certain disillusionment, their courage vanishes and the action collapses of itself.'[45] The First World War, and Social Democracy's response to it, served only to reinforce this element in Luxemburg's thinking. In 1918, she located the chief difficulty facing the struggle for socialism 'in the proletariat itself, in its lack of maturity or rather in the lack of maturity of its leaders, of the socialist parties'.[46] She had already by this time given her support to the idea of creating a new International whose decisions would be binding on each of the national sections.[47]

*   *   *

Against fifty years of accumulated misunderstanding, not all of it entirely innocent, it is worth setting the mature and considered judgements on Rosa Luxemburg of just two persons: Lenin and Trotsky. Neither delivered himself of an uncritical eulogy. But for both of them her name was that of a great revolutionary and not of a deviation. Lenin listed her errors: mistaken on the question of Poland, mistaken in 1903 in her appraisal of Menshevism, mistaken on the theory of capitalist accumulation, and so on; but he made no reference to any *systematic* error such as 'spontaneism' and her works, according to him, should serve as 'manuals for training many generations of Communists all over the world'.[48] For Trotsky,

[45] 'The Mass Strike, the Political Party and the Trade Unions', Waters, p. 190; 'The Next Step', Looker, p. 149; and cf. 'The Russian Revolution', Waters, pp. 372–4.

[46] 'Fragment sur la guerre etc.', *loc. cit.*, p. 99.

[47] See 'Theses on the Tasks of International Social Democracy', Waters, pp. 330–1.

[48] *Collected Works,* Vol. 33, p. 210. See also 'A Contribution to the History of the Question of the Dictatorship', Vol. 31, pp. 341–2. There Lenin, in speaking of the mass struggles of 1905 and the way they posed the question of revolutionary proletarian power, writes: 'Such outstanding representatives of the revolutionary proletariat and of unfalsified Marxism as Rosa Luxemburg immediately realised the significance of this practical experience.'

Luxemburg's counterposition of the spontaneity of mass actions to the bureaucratic apparatus of German Social Democracy had 'a thoroughly revolutionary and progressive character'; she never confined herself to it, did not develop 'the theory of spontaneity into a consummate metaphysics'; the most that could be said was that she did not put enough emphasis on 'the preparatory selection of the vanguard'.[49] Today we have to make our own assessment of Rosa Luxemburg. The one that has been made here follows those of Lenin and Trotsky in regarding her thought as an invaluable part of the tradition of revolutionary Marxism. It is a resource which cannot be co-opted to the service of bureaucratic organisations which fear proletarian democracy like the plague. Revolutionaries have less reason than anybody to squander their resources.

[49] 'Luxemburg and the Fourth International', *Writings of Leon Trotsky 1935–36*, New York 1970, p. 111.

Bourgeois Power and Socialist Democracy: On the Relation of Ends and Means

I

'To be regarded as successful, a revolution must be the achievement of something new. But violence and the effects of violence . . . are things only too familiar, too hopelessly unrevolutionary.'

Aldous Huxley[1]

An academic journal recently carried an article on Rosa Luxemburg in which her theory of revolution was not only counterposed to that of Lenin, a thing one has come to expect, but also annexed quite explicitly to an altogether non-Marxist and bourgeois tradition of thought.[2] The author of the article distinguishes himself in it not by the stringency of his methods of interpretation and not by the sureness of his grasp either of Luxemburg's thought in particular or of Marxism in general. Nor indeed is his enterprise entirely novel. Others before him have attempted to turn Luxemburg's words to uses and purposes as remote from her own. Take for instance these words from her critique of the Bolsheviks in 1918: 'Freedom only for the supporters of the government, only for the members of one party – however numerous they may be – is no freedom at all. Freedom is always and exclusively freedom for the one who thinks differently. Not because of any fanatical concept of "justice" but because all that is instruc-

---

[1] A. Huxley, *Ends and Means,* London 1937, p. 25.
[2] E. Vollrath, 'Rosa Luxemburg's Theory of Revolution', *Social Research,* Vol. 40, No. 1, Spring 1973, pp. 83–109. Page references to this article will be given in brackets in the text.

tive, wholesome and purifying in political freedom depends on this essential characteristic, and its effectiveness vanishes when "freedom" becomes a special privilege.'[3] When Bertram Wolfe, in an introduction to her pamphlet, cites this passage and adds 'Is there any regime which loves liberty which could not be proud to engrave these three sentences over the portals of its public buildings?', it is clear that his interests here are somewhat different from Luxemburg's and this not only from the piety of the formulation. Wolfe expressly wants to bury revolutionary Marxism ('hopelessly dated', 'dogmas which would not bear examination', etc.), but he wants to reclaim from it before doing so Luxemburg's 'love of liberty'.[4] The aforementioned article is also centrally concerned with liberty. It holds an interest in relation to predecessors such as this in being based on something more than tendentious quotation and ideological animus, though it is not free from these. What distinguishes it is a more or less coherent philosophical conception, from scrutiny of which it may be possible to learn something.

Now, of course, one cannot simply overlook the fact that Rosa Luxemburg was a Marxist, and the author, Ernst Vollrath, does make some token genuflections in its direction. Thus he acknowledges that she is 'a socialist thinker' in whose writings can be found such 'well-known socialist formulas' as 'the class struggle' (p. 90); that, in her view, 'the masses of the people remain excluded from active participation in political action [under] the conditions of capitalism' (p. 102), or, as he also says, the 'proletariat' is so excluded (pp. 90, 97); that it is precisely this proletariat that she regards as the agency of revolution (pp. 93, 98); and even that the 1918 critique of Lenin and Trotsky is presented 'under the Marxist formula of the dictatorship of the proletariat' (p. 103). However, if he still wishes to insist that Luxemburg's theory of revolution 'differs fundamentally' from that of Marx

[3] 'The Russian Revolution', M.-A. Waters (ed.), *Rosa Luxemburg Speaks*, New York 1970, pp. 389–90.
[4] 'Introduction' to R. Luxemburg, *The Russian Revolution, and Leninism or Marxism?*, Ann Arbor 1961, pp. 23–4.

(p. 85), he can only establish the existence of such a difference by effectively forgetting that these points have been made. For he simultaneously offers an interpretation of her theory from which the class struggle has been spirited away, to be replaced by the notion that the realm of universal freedom is the immediate and unproblematic product of revolution.

According to Vollrath, Luxemburg's concept of revolution 'corresponds completely to the modern non-Marxist concept', the classic formula for which was apparently given by Robespierre and consists in affirming that the aim of revolutionary government is to found the republic. But 'republic' being, as he tells us, 'the word for the realm of the free and public action of *all* men', it follows that the 'mission and the goal of revolution is to found the democratic republic as the realm of free action by *all* men' (pp. 94–5).⁵ It follows equally that when the author chances to remember that, for Luxemburg, this revolution is made by the proletariat, he has the latter conquering not power, let alone dictatorial power, but only 'a share in active self-determination' (pp. 96, 94). But he rarely does remember it. It soon turns out that *all* men are not only the revolution's beneficiaries but also its makers. Thus he can say in relation to Rosa Luxemburg: 'Just as the realm of a community of free men can be founded only if they will unite for spontaneous action in freedom, it can be maintained only if all of them will spontaneously act in freedom' (p. 101). Or again: 'The realm of the freedom of all, founded by the spontaneous action of all and maintained by the active spontaneity of all – this is what she calls "socialist democracy"' (p. 102). Further: 'The revolution, conceived as the process of all men coming to be active to establish the freedom of all, is continued and realised as all are active in freedom' (pp. 106–7). The 'cardinal question' of Luxemburg's

⁵ Emphases added. Cf. George Lichtheim who appears to take a similar view though judging it differently: 'her message was utopian, for a revolution which respects the liberty of *all* is the hardest thing in the world to achieve.' *The Concept of Ideology and Other Essays*, New York 1967, p. 203. Cf. also Hannah Arendt: 'she was alone . . . in her stress on the absolute necessity of not only individual but public freedom under *all* circumstances.' *Men in Dark Times*, London 1970, p. 52, emphasis added.

thought, predictably enough, here loses all trace of its speci-
ficity; it is not the mass strike, not even the proletarian
revolution, but 'how democracy . . . can be realised' and,
according to the author, 'the problem of the realisation of
democracy emergès everywhere and in all political systems'
(p. 93). The final consequence is that her thought, systematically differentiated by him from that of Marx and of Lenin,
is at the same time related in various ways to the ideas of
James Madison, Thomas Jefferson and Alexis de Tocqueville
(pp. 105–6).

It is worth pausing for a moment to note what exegetical
standards govern the production of these extraordinary
notions. As is evident from the few lines already cited,
Vollrath situates Luxemburg's thought in a region of eternal
harmonies wherein there appear to be no antagonistic interests,
no violent conflicts, no contradictions in the Marxist sense,
but only the unity of everyone in the achievement and
maintenance of freedom. All of this being, however, clearly
alien to the principal theses of historical materialism, he
does not shrink from opposing her to them. Thus, he feels
able 'to set her political thinking apart from that of Marx and
of orthodox Marxists, to whom politics is and remains an
estranged derivative of economics' (p. 90). Apparently, 'she
by no means shares Lenin's and Trotsky's view of the derivative character of the realm of state and politics' (p. 105). These
formulations of the materialist conception are hardly adequate
but that is not the point. The point is that the only specific
piece of evidence given in support of this claim – namely,
Luxemburg's insight into the reciprocal interaction of political
and economic factors during a revolutionary period[6] – in no
way 'suffices' (p. 90) to distinguish her from either Marx or
Lenin or Trotsky, to speak only of them. But then the author's
understanding of their approach to revolution leaves more
than a little to be desired. He writes, for example, that 'Rosa
Luxemburg expressly rejects the theory *worked out by Lenin,*
with its possibility of scheduling the revolution "for a certain

---

[6] See above pp. 120–1.

calendar day, by way of a central committee decision" – which would mean turning it into a "mere combat technique that might be 'decided upon' or possibly 'forbidden' at will, with the best of science and conscience"' (p. 88).[7] That he should take such a view of Lenin is not all that perplexing; but the quotations suggesting that she did are more so. It is true that her polemic of 1904 accuses Lenin of both Blanquism and subjectivism.[8] But could she really have thought that Lenin regarded revolution as a mere combat technique to be decided on or forbidden at will? The answer is that the lines Vollrath quotes are from Luxemburg's mass strike pamphlet and are directed against Bernstein, Bomelburg and the German trade union leaders, well-known Leninists they, for taking such an attitude towards the mass strike.[9] In any case, the contrast which the article most consistently sets up between Marxism on the one hand, and Rosa Luxemburg on the other, is the following: whereas in Marxist theory 'the realm of the state and of politics is determined . . . by the element of force [and] revolution can only mean the forcible . . . seizure of power' (p. 87), and whereas Lenin, for example, holds on to the 'identifications of politics and force, of state and force, of political action and force' (p. 89); Rosa Luxemburg, on the other hand, 'opposes . . . the seemingly so plausible identification of revolution and force', she 'distinguishes revolution from pure use of force' (p. 88); she 'expressly questions Lenin's basic thesis – taken from Marx, but implied from the outset in the modern state concept – that the state and the politics identified with the state are nothing but instrumentalities of oppression and class rule' (p. 102).

Tedious though it may be to do so, we will expose the emptiness of this contrast. Vollrath's article is, after all, only a more consistent and thoroughgoing attempt to do with Rosa Luxemburg what an assortment of Social-Democrats and

[7] Emphasis added.

[8] See 'Organisational Questions of Russian Social Democracy', Waters, pp. 118, 130.

[9] See 'The Mass Strike, the Political Party and the Trade Unions', Waters, pp. 158–9.

bourgeois ideologues have been trying to do sporadically for fifty years – namely, to oppose her belief in 'democracy' to the necessity of proletarian revolution. It is therefore worth uncovering not only the theory which guides it but also the method it requires. The claim that Luxemburg rejects the identification of state and revolution with force is supported with two things, a sentence and a page reference. In the sentence, revolution is said by her to be something other and more than bloodshed. Its context, omitted in the article, is this: 'When . . . the representatives of our German opportunism hear of '[revolution", they immediately think of bloodshed, street fighting or powder and shot, and the logical conclusion thereof is: the mass strike leads inevitably to the revolution, therefore we dare not have it. In actual fact we see in Russia that almost every mass strike in the long run leads to an encounter with the armed guardians of Tsarist order. . . . The revolution, however, is something other and something more than bloodshed. In contradiction to the police interpretation, which views the revolution exclusively from the standpoint of street disturbances and rioting, that is . . . of "disorder" – the interpretation of scientific socialism sees in the revolution above all a thoroughgoing internal reversal of social class relations.'[10] Limiting ourselves only to the source which the author himself chose to cite, we see that for Luxemburg, while the revolution is indeed not just bloodshed and 'disorder', it does involve encounters with the armed organs of the state and hence force. So, where is the contrast with Marx or Lenin on this score? Perhaps, in referring to their identification of revolution with force, he wishes to suggest that for them revolution is nothing but force, nothing more or other than bloodshed. If so, he will labour for many years and in vain to find some confirmation of that.

The page reference fares no better. It is evidently to the following passage: 'Lenin says: the bourgeois state is an instrument of oppression of the working class; the socialist state, of the bourgeoisie. To a certain extent, he says, it is

[10] *ibid.*, p. 186.

only the capitalist state stood on its head. This simplified view misses the most essential thing; bourgeois class rule has no need of the political training and education of the entire mass of the people, at least not beyond certain narrow limits. But for the proletarian dictatorship that is the life element, the very air without which it is not able to exist.'[11] These lines are supposed to back the claim that the Marxist and Leninist thesis on the state is 'absolutely unacceptable to Rosa Luxemburg' (p. 102), that 'she considers obsolete [the] identifications of the political realm with violence and domination' (pp. 105–6). But, limiting ourselves again only to the source cited, they show nothing of the kind. She draws attention to a crucial difference between two forms of class rule without in any way suggesting that they cease thereby to be forms of *class rule*. Obviously, she does not regard the state as 'nothing but' (p. 102) an instrument of oppression. Vollrath is right if that is all he wants to say. But he is ignorant and wrong to maintain that the orthodox Marxist thesis as understood by Lenin amounts to such a view. The most cursory glance at *The State and Revolution* will confirm not only that Lenin envisages tasks for the proletarian dictatorship other than those of class oppression, but also incidentally that he is well aware of, and himself stresses, the difference to which Luxemburg draws attention, so that this particular criticism of hers is misdirected. Here again, then, in relation to the state as in relation to revolution, the contrast which Vollrath wishes to sustain collapses. In Marxist theory, both state and revolution are more than just vehicles of force and class rule. The contrast could only have gained credibility from some evidence, which he is unable to produce, that for Luxemburg they are *not at all* vehicles of force and class rule. This brings us to the heart of the matter. For while he never says that in so many words, nevertheless in the ruins of his attempt at an interpretation of her thought can be found the structure of philosophical argument which entails it.

What the argument says is that the end of revolution is by

[11] 'The Russian Revolution', Waters, p. 389.

its very nature such that it cannot be achieved with the use of means which are distinct from it (p. 93). In a nutshell: the realm of free action must be founded by free action. The end must be expressed within the means of achieving it as a kind of immanent presence there. In fact, as we shall see, it is no accident that one of the most convenient ways of stating the thesis is in a terminology of strongly spiritual flavour. Even the linguistic/conceptual dichotomy of ends and means is rejected by the author as inadequate to the problems of revolution because it lends itself to a model of instrumental rationality in which that relationship of immanence is called into question. In this model there can be means (of production, for example) which are and remain quite distinct from the end (the product), and which are both necessary to producing it and dispensable once it has been produced. 'According to [the] common Marxist conviction,' Vollrath writes, 'revolution is a means to an end that is altogether different from revolution. Yet any means-end relationship takes its bearings from the model of making things' (p. 86). We can correct this characterisation of the Marxist conviction later. What is important here is that for the model of making, with its implication of objectively ascertainable relationships between discrete entities, he substitutes a philosophy of voluntary action which brings into play only the actor and his purposes marrying them together in a perfect harmony.

According to this philosophy, 'all action is a beginning, a new beginning of something which previously did not exist' (p. 83) and 'posits a difference from all that has gone before' (p. 84). Revolution, as 'the start of free action on the part of those who were not freely active before' (p. 98), represents just such a new beginning, and it appears to be governed by its purpose alone. For, the revolution's purpose is freedom: 'The point of revolutionary activity is the constitution of the realm of freedom' (p. 105); and the revolution itself is a manifestation of freedom: 'The community of free men is established by acting in freedom' (p. 98); and whether one is talking about the purpose achieved, in the shape of a free community, or about the act of achieving it, in the shape of revolution, the substance is one and the same – in Vollrath's own words: 'The freedom of action is the sole determining principle of both moments' (p. 101); 'Both the foundation and the continuing preservation of the freedom to act are basically identical, going back to one principle: to freedom, to the self-determining action of all' (p. 106). From here to his interpretation of Rosa Luxemburg the way is clear.

II

'Or say that the end precedes the beginning,
And the end and the beginning were always there
Before the beginning and after the end.
And all is always now.'

T. S. Eliot[12]

The argument we have uncovered is idealist to the very core. Between ends and means in the revolutionary process it stipulates a type of unity which can be described simultaneously as both spiritual and organic. Were it only that this argument had been used to shore up a careless interpretation of Luxemburg's work in the spirit of liberalism, it would not be of significant interest. However, there is a theme encountered frequently in the writings of a more revolutionary tradition – of socialists and, especially, of anarchists – which is at the very least ambiguous, and one of whose meanings appears to call for the same type of unity between ends and means. Generally, what is more, this theme displays a concern which can be impatiently brushed aside today by no honest and serious revolutionary. If the theme has a name, it is probably that of *prefiguration*. In any case, the thought has often been expressed: in the struggle for liberation the end must be prefigured or anticipated by, reflected or adumbrated in, the means employed to secure it.

Some may be inclined to detect that thought within the

---

[12] T. S. Eliot, *Four Quartets*, London 1959, p. 19.

Marxist principle of proletarian self-emancipation. In revolutionary Marxism, however, the latter principle has been complementary to the notion of the dictatorship of the proletariat. It has been the anarchist tradition, waging a long historical controversy against Marxism, that has consistently challenged the attempt to approach the ultimate abolition of political authority via its temporary, or transitional, use. The anarchist tradition has challenged also what it saw as, and of, authoritarianism within political organisations that were, or claimed to be, Marxist. Already in the disputes in the First International, the supporters of Bakunin had thrown down this challenge. 'How,' they asked, 'can a free and egalitarian society arise from an authoritarian organisation? It is impossible. The International embodies future human society. . . .'[13] Ever since 1917, anarchist writers have continued to voice the same kind of objection against the Leninist concept of the vanguard. It is no accident then if, at a higher level of abstraction, the theme of a necessary harmony between means and ends has remained an integral part of this libertarian current of thought. That theme has been eloquently restated in recent years by at least two writers, one himself an anarchist, the other a socialist concerned to emphasise anarchism's contemporary relevance. These two restatements can serve as a convenient point of departure for the discussion which follows.

The American anarchist, Murray Bookchin, in a stimulating and passionately argued book which ranges over questions of ecology, technology and revolutionary strategy, puts the matter thus: 'Like the movement in which he participates, the revolutionist must try to reflect the conditions of the society he is trying to achieve – at least to the degree that this is possible today. The treacheries and failures of the past half century have made it axiomatic that there *can be no separation of the revolutionary process from the revolutionary goal*. . . . A libertarian society can be achieved only by a libertarian revolution.'[14] Behind the one qualifying phrase suggesting

---

[13] Cited in M. Evans, *Karl Marx,* London 1975, p. 44.

[14] M. Bookchin, *Post-Scarcity Anarchism,* London 1974, pp. 45–6.

that there are limits on what is immediately possible, there lie concealed the whole weakness of anarchism, all its logical contradictions and, in particular, the material implications which overturn the so-called axiom. There *must be* some separation between the process and the goal. But we limit ourselves for the moment simply to exhibiting the prefiguration theme. It recurs in Bookchin's argument. The revolutionary group, he tells us, must constitute itself in accordance with the (decentralised) organisational principles of the society it seeks to achieve, the revolutionary movement be 'congruent' with that society. The Marxist 'revolutionary party', on the contrary, he sees as embodying (hierarchical) principles *'that reflect the very society it professes to oppose'*. At stake in this dichotomy he insists, invoking the prospect of catastrophe, is not merely the realisation of freedom, but everything: 'Listen, Marxist: The organisation we try to build is the kind of society our revolution will create. Either we will shed the past – in ourselves as well as in our groups – or there will simply be no future to win.'[15] The second writer, Anthony Arblaster, while being critical of the anarchist tradition on certain important points, emphatically supports it in the matter under discussion, and arguments strikingly similar to Bookchin's make their appearance in a recent article by him on the subject of anarchism. He there states, rightly no doubt, that some of the characteristically anarchist themes have become more generally pervasive on the New Left, and mentions in particular the idea 'that the kind of society which only a revolution can produce can nevertheless be foreshadowed, demonstrated, shown in miniature in the personal behaviour of revolutionaries and in the kind of institutions they create.' He himself upholds the need for 'a consistency between means and ends, not simply for some general moral reason, but because it is in practice impossible to separate means from ends'. As he goes on to explain: 'If we want finally to win for ourselves a fully free and democratic society,

---

[15] *ibid.*, pp. 48, 196, 220. According to Bookchin the alternative confronting us, 'more drastic' than socialism-or-barbarism, is 'anarchism or annihilation' (p. 40).

those same principles will have to be embodied in the struggle for it, and in the agencies of that struggle. The costs of separating the future from the present, means from ends, present necessities from the ultimate utopia, have already been commented on. The last devastating cost of this disjunctic.ı ıs that it guarantees that utopia will never be reached.'[16]

The theme of prefiguration, then, is readily identifiable by reference to the anarchist tradition. However, something similar is occasionally also found, hinted at by way of metaphor, in revolutionary Marxist writing. 'Seeds of wheat must be sown in order to yield an ear of wheat.' Thus does Trotsky, for example, formulate the interdependence of means and ends in *Their Morals and Ours*. He also quotes some lines from a play by Lassalle which admonish us to point out not only the goal but also the path, given the intimate relationship which exists between the two.[17] The same metaphor of travel finds its way into some lines Rosa Luxemburg herself wrote in 1918 during the German revolution, lines by the way which should give Ernst Vollrath pause: 'The path of the revolution follows clearly from its ends, its method follows from its task. All power in the hands of the working masses, in the hands of the workers' and soldiers' councils . . . this is the guiding principle. . . . Every step, every act . . . must, like a compass, point in this direction.'[18] In addition, we have shown in the preceding essay how Luxemburg, during the early years of the century, stressed continually the need for the day-to-day struggle to embody, or be informed by, the revolutionary socialist goal. This was her way, inadequate as we argued, of insisting that the revolutionary conquest of power be taken seriously by the German Social-Democratic

[16] A. Arblaster, 'The Relevance of Anarchism', in R. Miliband and J. Saville (eds.), *The Socialist Register 1971*, London 1971, pp. 168–9, 177–8; and cf., by the same writer, 'Liberal Values and Socialist Values', in R. Miliband and J. Saville (eds.), *The Socialist Register 1972*, London 1972, p. 97.

[17] L. Trotsky *et al., Their Morals and Ours*, New York 1966, p. 42.

[18] 'The Beginning', R. Looker (ed.), *Rosa Luxemburg : Selected Political Writings*, London 1972, p. 254.

movement, be treated by it as a *real* objective.[19] And indeed
it is hardly surprising if, notwithstanding the differences
between Marxism and anarchism on the nature of revolution
and revolutionary strategy, formulations like the above are
present in Marxist writing. For the theme of prefiguration
which they too suggest can be construed in a way which is not
merely unobjectionable from a Marxist point of view, but in
fact entirely uncontroversial, so obviously true as to seem at
first quite trivial. Seeds of wheat must be sown: absolutely, for
if you sow dragons' teeth you don't get wheat. The obvious
truth here is that the accomplishment of an end requires that
the means used really be means to that end. This can be
expressed from one angle by saying that means determine
ends, in the sense that actual outcomes are dependent on the
objective consequences of the means used. It can be expressed
from another angle by saying that ends determine means, in
the sense that means used must be chosen with a view to the
likelihood of their being able to produce the projected ends.
But, however expressed, the point is unlikely to provoke
dissent. That means determine ends is affirmed by people of
quite sundry persuasions: not only by Anthony Arblaster[20]
from a position sympathetic to, but detached from, Marxism,
but also by Trotsky; and not only by the American philo-
sopher, John Dewey, who, challenging Trotsky as to whether
the class struggle is the only agency of human liberation,
nevertheless agreed with him in defending the principle that
the end justifies the means;[21] but also by Aldous Huxley who
explicitly rejected that same principle in his self-styled
'practical cookery book of reform'.[22] The differences only
begin when the substantive issues of history and politics are
posed: what *are* the objective consequences of the different
political and strategic options available?

Even if, however, the objective interdependence of means

[19] See above pp. 114–16.

[20] 'The Relevance of Anarchism', *loc. cit.*, p. 177.

[21] L. Trotsky *et al., op. cit.*, pp. 40–3, 55–60, and L. Trotsky, *The Permanent
Revolution & Results and Prospects*, London 1962, p. 88.

[22] Huxley, *op. cit.*, p. 9.

and ends is obvious, it may not be altogether trivial to draw attention to the obvious in this case. For, all too often, in practice, what is done supposedly as a means toward some end is done merely *in its name* without any too careful attention being given to what might be the real aim in, or consequence of, adopting such means. Leave aside the depravities committed against the Vietnamese people, for instance, in the name of defending its freedom, or against the Chilean masses, for another, in the name of the principle that 'Man is the end of all societies': it is not the purpose of this essay to 'debate' what is the real aim of their perpetrators and apologists. Be it the freedom of action of American imperial power, the freedom of private property, or only the freedom for Chicago economists to debase themselves utterly by the pleasure they take at the allegedly small 'cost' of rescuing Chile from 'economic chaos',[23] this aim is in any case separated by a clear line of demarcation from the goal of liberation central to the revolutionary socialist project. But unfortunately – tragically – the cause of revolutionary socialism itself has suffered incalculable harm through insufficient scrutiny having been devoted by so many of its adherents to the question of just how, for example, by the silencing of critical thought and the systematic cultivation of lies, or just how by the murder of revolutionaries and the perfection of the instruments of police control, the goal of socialism is brought nearer. All of this has been, needless to say, a phenomenon more complex than moral turpitude. It drew strength from the tendency to regard the ultimate goals of the socialist movement as, in some sort, a metaphysical certainty, guaranteed by the infallible wisdom of the 'leadership' or by the inexorable laws of history, lodged within a future which no present action or crime could compromise. To that extent, one of the concerns at the heart of the prefiguration theme, the concern to stress that means determine ends, is more than justified. Socialism is the goal of *our* time; whether it will be

[23] See M. Chossudovsky, 'Chicago Economics, Chilean Style', *Monthly Review*, Vol. 26, No. 11, April 1975, pp. 14–7.

reached and, if so, the shape it takes, will be directly affected by the movements of our time and what they do.

However, the argument we have chosen to isolate, both in the article by Ernst Vollrath and by reference to a long libertarian tradition, goes a good deal beyond this in speaking of the *identity/inseparability* of means and ends: freedom is both means and end; the organisation we build *is* the kind of society we want to create; there must be congruence or consistency between movement and goal, means and end. There is something extremely odd, to say the least, in the form of this argument. For, were the relationship involved a true identity, then the problem to which the argument addresses itself, the problem broadly speaking of revolutionary strategy, would cease to exist. Either the means of a struggle for socialism are already available and so therefore is the end, in which case there cannot be a revolutionary *process* since socialism is instantaneously realisable and realised; or socialism is not instantaneously realisable, the end therefore does not yet exist and *ex hypothesi* there are no means available with which to struggle for it. This is, of course, an extreme and ridiculous caricature, though even in this form it evokes certain real libertarian positions, in particular, maximalist and abstentionist ones. But the point is that it is arrived at by taking the identity argument at its word. This is not the way in which its proponents mean it to be taken. For, in the same breath with which the identity/inseparability of means and ends is affirmed it is also denied. The burden of performing this simultaneous affirmation and denial is carried by precisely that array of terms in which the means/end relationship is typically formulated: the end is prefigured, anticipated or foreshadowed by, reflected, embodied or expressed in, the means with which it is achieved. Each of these terms announces that the means are not yet the end. But lest we be tempted to conclude from this that they are, then, in some measure distinct and separate from it, and not fully congruent or harmonious with it, and must in fact obey other necessities than just utopia, each term also forbids that dislocation. The means, it tells us, do still 'match' the end in some way, albeit one difficult to articulate clearly. They are cast in its image or partake of its substance; although they are not it, it is in part contained within or immanent to them.[24] These ideas are one-sided and therefore false. Let us consider what models might lend them a clear and articulate meaning.

The first is a metaphor familiar by now. Means and end in the struggle for socialism are related to one another as the seed of wheat to the mature plant. In a sense, the two are obviously different. In another sense, they are not, because they are connected together by a process of natural growth, constitute, that is to say, the same entity but at two different stages of its development. The seed is not yet a plant. However, it can become a plant. Embryonically this future stage of its growth is already contained within it. The difference and distinction between means and end are here subsumed within a broader unity whose type is *organic*, and it is precisely an organic unity between them, such as prevents for example the seed of wheat from turning into a radish, which can give material sense to the idea that means must prefigure their ends, as well as to the further idea, which this one presupposes, that they are able unambiguously to do so. However, such sense is only gained at the cost of overlooking all those equally material factors which would have to be taken into account if this metaphor was to be even remotely serviceable as an analogy for a real historical process. For the production of wheat, seeds of wheat are never in fact sufficient. On hard and barren ground, for instance, plough and fertilisers are also needed and these are as much means of production of wheat as is the seed. But a plough is not a seed of wheat, does not contain wheat, not even in germ, cannot become wheat. Wheat is no more already present in it than is a statue in uncut marble or a sketch on blank canvas. To say in these

---

[24] In a previous discussion of Trotsky and Luxemburg, we ourselves wrongly conflated the obvious point about means having to *effect* ends with more dubious and unilateral formulations of this kind – 'The content of the future must already be sketched in the activity of the present', 'the end must already be operative in the means employed' – whose ultimate meaning can only be an idealist one. See N. Geras, 'Political Participation in the Revolutionary Thought of Leon Trotsky', in G. Parry (ed.), *Participation in Politics*, Manchester 1972, pp. 164–6.

cases that the end is prefigured by or embodied in the means can have no sense, save that the plough is after all a means of production of wheat or that marble and canvas are needed for the execution of sculpture and sketch respectively. In that event, the idea of prefiguration is reduced to the obvious truth which has already been conceded to it. The plough, just because it is not organically related to the various ends which it can be used to produce, is a more neutral means than the seed. Moreover, the soil which in its hard and barren state constitutes the material point of departure in this example is not even neutral with regard to the production of wheat, but actually resistant to that end until it has been suitably transformed. So transformed, it embodies some of the preconditions for producing wheat. However, in the first instance it also embodies obstacles.

If all of this draws attention to the fact that the relationship between means and ends is a more complex, less harmonious and more problematic one than is stipulated in the prefiguration theme, it may also serve to indicate why that should be so. Earlier a sense was defined in which ends can be said to determine means. But a certain care must be taken with this notion lest the problem of revolutionary strategy be taken for a kind of metaphysical teleology. The sense in question was that the means must be chosen with a view to their capacity to *effect* the relevant ends, and the very reference to effectivity invokes a context of material causality, an objective reality which forms the point of departure from which those ends are to be produced. The nature of the objective reality participates, so to speak, with the nature of the ends in view, causalities with finalities, in determining the character of the means. If these means 'reflect' anything at all, they will certainly reflect that reality. Thus, where the seed of wheat in the above example shows something about the projected end, the fertilisers show something about the state of the soil. The direction of a road, by change of metaphor, is determined not only by its point of destination but also by its point of departure and by such points, such obstacles, as may have to be avoided on the way. The road obviously tends toward, and ultimately reaches, its destination, but being determined by points other than that one alone, it is not identical with it and passes through points that are quite separate from it. The theme of prefiguration is one-sided in much the same way as was the metaphor of organic growth in its initial form, falls victim to the same simplification. It abstracts from the objective reality which is the irreducibly given, if changing, point of origin and focuses exclusively on the nature of the projected end. On this basis, and only on this basis, which transforms the end itself into the origin – first principle and source of all others – is it possible to insist that the means must express the end. For an end abstracted from material reality is a project without objective preconditions or limits, a project whose every aspect must express its purpose since it is governed only by that purpose, indeed *is* that purpose. The only process which meets these demanding criteria is that of pure and original creation, hence *the* Act of Creation or, perhaps, the March of God in the World.

In this precisely we confront the second model which gives sense, a spiritual sense now, to the idea of prefiguration. It is the model of what Althusser has called a spiritual or expressive totality[25] and, as it concerns us here, it relates the end to the means in the struggle for socialism as the purpose to its creations. As in the first model, so here, there is the doubled relationship of identity/difference established between the purpose and its means of actualisation. In an initial moment, the purpose is different from the creation, the end from the means, distinguishable from it in the shape of pure subjectivity. But a subject without objects, a purpose without works, is good for nothing; to be actualised it must objectify itself in its creations. In a second moment, it is therefore the same as these creations, because it is realised by them as its means, objectified and manifest in them. Again, no single aspect of the whole creation, no particular means, can be identical with the purpose, since the latter only realises itself in the

[25] See L. Althusser, *For Marx*, London 1969, pp. 101–4, 202–4, and L. Althusser and E. Balibar, *Reading Capital*, London 1970, pp. 93–7.

whole. But relating to the purpose as the part to the whole, each aspect and means of its realisation must at least partake of its being or share something of its essence. In this case, then, the difference and distinction between means and end are subsumed within a unity whose type is *spiritual,* and it is precisely a spiritual unity between them which preserves their marriage in perfect harmony against the demands and the conflicts of a more mundane necessity. From a materialist point of view what is wrong with this model, baldly stated, is that in favour of a purpose it abolishes the world. Those, however, who hope to act effectively in the world cannot fashion their means in ignorance of its realities as if these did not exist, for every real creation, even the most inspired, is subject to dictates other than the will of its creator. Labour is not the only source of wealth; nature is too. Men make history but in circumstances that are given and not chosen.

It may appear to be excessive even beyond the point of caricature to visit a metaphysic of pure creation upon the writers whose arguments have been examined. We are concerned, however, not at all with what the ultimate metaphysical commitments of these writers might be, only with what conception of revolution their arguments regarding means and ends presuppose; and that is a conception which treats revolution *as if* it were a process of pure creation. It surfaces most clearly in Vollrath's case: here there is a leap into the realm of freedom, a leap which is quite explicitly self-propelled, self-directed and unlimited, not grounded in other words in any realm of necessity. We have seen already how he defines the freedom of action as the 'sole determining principle' of the revolutionary process, and action itself as a new beginning that 'posits a difference from all that has gone before'. Significantly, he begins his article with these lines from Cicero which he sees as encapsulating that doctrine of action: 'For there is nothing in which human faculties come closer to the power of the gods than either founding new states or maintaining those already founded' (p. 83). Such invocation of the gods could, of course, be merely a loose way of talking, but in fact there is many another passage to testify that it is not. Vollrath writes for example: 'Unlike, indeed in contrast to, mere behaviour – which is subject to norms of behavioral biology, depth psychology, sociology or economics, is uniform and accordingly fixed and confined – politically revolutionary action is free from these norms and restrictions, is diverse and unlimited. The circumstances it creates and in which it moves are precisely not fixed, confined, and restricted as are the ones of behaviour; *they are determined by action and counteraction alone*' (p. 95); 'This free action . . . *has only one goal:* to keep restoring its own possibility as free action' (p. 96); 'Revolutions are not made like things, at one stroke, but over a period of time in which the revolutionary activity must never cease, *lest the action vanish in a result that lies outside the action*' (p. 97);[26] and so forth. That such voluntarism, to all appearances wild and irrepressible, can be comfortably integrated within a perspective that is reformist through and through is a story we shall return to in the next section, one at least as old as Eduard Bernstein who, albeit in more sober form, could appeal against materialism to the Kantian ideal in order to liquidate socialism in a reformed capitalism.

Within the anarcho-libertarian problematic the model of pure creation or, what is the same thing, of the new beginning in wholesale negation of the past, is less consistently present, but only because its proponents adhere less consistently than does Vollrath to the theme of a harmony between means and ends; and this for the very good reason that, despite their contempt for political 'realism', certain realities of the revolutionary process do from time to time intrude upon their vision. At such times, as we shall see, the prefiguration theme is generally forgotten. Nevertheless, the politics of anarchism are governed to an important degree by that theme, and, to the degree that they are, they too presuppose a model of pure creation and pure negation. What other model could justify the notions that the revolutionary movement must 'reflect' its goal *in contradistinction to* its point of departure,

[26] Emphases added.

that it must, or can, simply 'shed' the past, that it might be able to reach the 'ultimate utopia' without having to confront 'present necessities' quite distinct from that utopia? What all of these ideas overlook, to state only the bare minimum, is the brute fact of bourgeois power. This fact refuses to be spirited away even when it is the spirit of freedom and democracy that is abroad. It defies that spirit as also all other dreams of reconciliation. It is a reality which *lives*. To conclude this section, as we began, with the words of T. S. Eliot:

> '. . . but that which is only living
> Can only die . . .'[27]

III

'Socialism, both in its ends and in its means, is a struggle to realise freedom'.   Karl Korsch[28]

'A revolution is certainly the most authoritarian thing there is'.
Friedrich Engels[29]

In the idealised forms which they assume when in dispute with revolutionary Marxism, both anarchism and Social-Democratic reformism insist on a harmony between the purpose or spirit of liberation and the work of realising it. In reality neither of them is quite so pure. Anarchism in struggle, in Russia and in Spain, armed itself. Reformism in power, from Berlin in 1919 to Belfast now, has gotten blood on its hands. In or out of power, from the First World War to the war in Vietnam, it has given its blessing and its support to violence on a truly spectacular scale. This contrast – Marxism's old *tu quoque* – with the myth the two traditions have in common forms an indispensable back-drop to what follows, since this concerns itself largely with the myth: an emphasis on consistency between means and ends which accounts for

[27] Eliot, *loc. cit.*
[28] K. Korsch, *Marxism and Philosophy,* London 1970, p. 126.
[29] 'On Authority', K. Marx and F. Engels, *Selected Works,* 3 vols., Moscow 1969, Vol. 2, p. 379.

a certain structural homology between reformism and anarchism as ideologies. The juxtaposition of them here is not an *equation* nor, to be absolutely explicit on this point, is it an attempt to suggest, in the manner beloved of a whole Stalinist and post-Stalinist tradition, that anarchism is 'objectively' the same as reformism, 'objectively' counter-revolutionary, etc. There is a crucial difference between the two tendencies, one which is qualitative because it corresponds to the line that, in every critical situation, separates revolution *from* counter-revolution. The pursuit of consistency, the unity and the continuity between the process and the goal of liberation, are situated by anarchism beyond, and by reformism within, the boundary of the bourgeois state.

Yet just the unilateral placement of them (beyond *or* within) is what secures, in the myth, the unity and continuity against having to be broken by any coercive act. For the boundary is the problem. Itself policed by an apparatus of coercion which in normal circumstances, does not always observe even the canons and procedures of existing legality, and in critical ones, is capable, with the assistance of extra-state groups and organisations, of orgies of 'undisguised savagery and lawless revenge',[30] this boundary represents an obstacle in the way of human liberation. It represents the power of capital. For socialism to be achieved, such resistance as the latter has to offer must be overcome, such forces (people!) as it can mobilise in its defence must be politically defeated, the whole apparatus of coercion must be destroyed. Only by supposing that none of this does constitute an obstacle, or a serious obstacle, can the aforementioned harmony and continuity be preserved against disruption. In different ways both reformism and anarchism make that supposition.

For the first, the bourgeois state, insofar as it is democratic, represents not the power of capital but the principle of universality. In other words it is not a *bourgeois* state. Since reformism's ideal ends (democracy/liberty) are already contained by it, at least as principles, as forms in search of content,

---

[30] The expression is Marx's – 'The Civil War in France', *ibid.*, Vol. 2, p. 235.

as seeds that will bear fruit, its death is not required. On the contrary, it is through its life and growth, via the development and extension into new areas of the principles it embodies, that the power of capital is curbed. This is the triumph of persuasion and of compromise, of reconciliation – in a word, of reason over power. The polity in question turns out to be nothing less than the realm of freedom and the entry into the latter nothing more than the activity of the masses within the former. Socialism becomes the continuation and actualisation of liberalism, connected to it as it were organically, but connected also spiritually because presided over by the same benign ideals. For anarchism, the bourgeois state, as a state, is the paradigm of coercion and authoritarianism, these features of it being focused on to the virtual exclusion of all others. As such, it is the very antithesis of anarchism's ideal ends (liberty/equality) and its death is required. However, it is the essence of anarchism's libertarian ethic and theory that the destructive act involved here (as well as the destruction of capitalist relations which anarchism in its communist variants requires) must not be and need not be a coercive act. It must not and need not entail any recourse by the revolutionary movement either to action within the structures of the existing state or to the creation of an alternative form of political authority. That is to say – at least insofar as the ethic and the theory are adhered to – that the power to be destroyed can be so destroyed without ever having to be confronted on a common terrain with common weapons, those precisely of power; and that, in turn, is surely to say that its capacity for resistance and opposition is negligible, that before the triumphant ideals of libertarianism it simply ceases to be a power. In the perspective of anarchism there is, of course, a sharp break between past and future in a way that for reformism there is not because the revolutionary transformation does not disappear there into a long, drawn out and ever so gradual series of small changes. But this break disrupts only the chronology. At a deeper level, the revolutionary process is seen, in the same perspective, as unbroken and continuous. The Great Refusal begins here and now in the conduct of revolutionaries and comes to fruition in the anarchist utopia. Because the whole process takes place simply *beyond* the existing structures of authority and repression, which the movement resolutely shuns, its origin and its term can be united in a common respect for the same ideals; the anarchist group or milieu becomes a little germ of utopia. In Murray Bookchin's words:

'. . . subcultures begin to emerge which emphasise a natural diet as against the society's synthetic diet, an extended family as against the monogamous family, sexual freedom as against sexual repression, tribalism as against atomisation, community as against urbanism, mutual aid as against competition, communism as against property, and, finally, anarchism as against hierarchy and the state. In the very act of refusing to live by bourgeois strictures, the first seeds of the utopian lifestyle are planted. Negation passes into affirmation; the rejection of the present becomes the assertion of the future within the rotting guts of capitalism itself. "Dropping out" becomes a mode of dropping in – into the tentative, experimental, and as yet highly ambiguous, social relations of utopia. Taken as an end in itself, this lifestyle is not utopia; indeed, it may be woefully incomplete. Taken as a means, however, this lifestyle . . . [is] indispensable in remaking the revolutionary, in awakening his sensibilities to how much must be changed if the revolution is to be complete . . . in preserving the integrity of the revolutionary, in providing him with the psychic resources to resist the subversion of the revolutionary project by bourgeois values.'[31]

[31] Bookchin, *op. cit.*, p. 16. It is indicative of the more general problem being discussed here that amongst the bourgeois values permeating the socialist project and the traditional left Bookchin places not only hierarchy, sexism, puritanism, not only the 'work ethic', but also 'renunciation' (pp. 13, 47). Coming from a revolutionary, that is an insult, though one wholly in keeping with the idealist core of his argument, to the sacrifices, in many cases total and final, which literally countless oppressed people *had* to make in struggling against and living with their oppression – sacrifices, moreover, which are still being made daily as part of a continuing, life-and-death tragedy, 'post-scarcity anarchism' and the 'sweeping affirmation of sensuousness' (p. 27) notwithstanding.

In their own ways, both reformism and anarchism dissolve the realities of bourgeois power before the ideal of liberation, a dissolution needless to say that is purely ideological. Reformism does it in order to preserve the reality against the ideal; it never transcends the capitalist present. Anarchism does it in order to preserve its ideal against the reality; it always 'anticipates' the libertarian future. Rosa Luxemburg has been claimed as both democrat *tout court* and libertarian. We shall take a closer look at what separates her from both of these idealist reductions.

The key to the interpretation of Luxemburg's thought with which this essay began is provided by the standard socialist formula, employed occasionally by her, in which a distinction is drawn between the democratic *form* of bourgeois parliamentary institutions and their class and inegalitarian *content*. Ernst Vollrath refers to one such use of this formula (p. 90), and on the basis of it proceeds to define as the fundamental question of her thought that concerning how democracy can be realised, 'not only in line with the concept, but by the activity of all' (p. 93). However, for him this is clearly a question as to how the difference between form and content can be ironed out, so to speak, as to how, more precisely, the existing democratic forms can be given a more suitable, i.e. democratic, content. The rest follows as night after day. The 'political realm' of which these democratic forms are constitutive is defined, following Kant, as 'a union of free men' (p. 90). Although in the first instance this is only formally a realm of freedom because the proletarian masses are effectively excluded from it by their conditions of existence, nevertheless they can by their 'revolutionary' activity win their own participation within it, thus conquer 'a share in self-determining action' (pp. 93–4). Despite all talk about the new beginning and about the diverse and unlimited character of revolutionary action, this latter appears in the end to be limited in a very specific way: it is in fact no different from political action in general (p. 96), and Luxemburg's 'socialist democracy is simply active participation by the masses in political life' (p. 102). Across 'the revolution' the continuity is thereby preserved of 'representative democracy as the political constitution of those who act in freedom' (p. 105). The gods as usual reconcile one to what exists. The relevant passage from Luxemburg's writings will be cited in a moment: but it is not difficult to show that by his gloss on her use of the distinction between democratic form and class content, Vollrath succeeds almost perfectly in uncovering the set of assumptions to be found in the thought . . . of Eduard Bernstein.

Embodied therein, above all, is this same notion of a fundamental institutional continuity through the transformation of capitalism into socialism: 'The liberal organisations of modern society . . . are flexible, and capable of change and development. They do not need to be destroyed, but only to be further developed.' If this is so for Bernstein, it is on the basis precisely that these organisations are already, in form, or in principle, or embryonically, egalitarian and socialist ones, so that by their development and completion – their only true inadequacy being that they are not yet complete – the inequalities and contradictions of capitalist society are gradually eradicated. This is a thought he expresses repeatedly and in different ways: 'Democracy is in principle the suppression of class government, though it is not yet the actual suppression of classes. . . . The right to vote in a democracy makes its members virtually partners in the community, and this virtual partnership must in the end lead to real partnership. . . . Universal suffrage is only a part of democracy, although a part which in time must draw the other parts after it as the magnet attracts to itself the scattered portions of iron.'[32] As Lucio Colletti has pointed out, the central axis on which Bernstein's thought turns and which accounts for this type of argument is the assumption of an incompatibility between political democracy and juridical equality, on the one hand, and social inequality and capitalist economic relations, on the other.[33] From this disharmony it

---

[32] E. Bernstein, *Evolutionary Socialism,* New York 1961, pp. 163, 143–5.

[33] See the lucid treatment of this question in L. Colletti, *From Rousseau to Lenin,* London 1972, pp. 51, 92–7, 103–8.

follows that every extension of democracy is automatically an erosion of capitalism. Revolution therefore ceases, in this definitive statement of the Social-Democratic creed, to be necessary: capitalism 'becomes' socialism.

'In all advanced countries we see the privileges of the capitalist bourgeoisie yielding step by step to democratic organisations. Under the influence of this, and driven by the movement of the working classes which is daily becoming stronger, a social reaction has set in against the exploiting tendencies of capital, a counteraction which, although it still proceeds timidly and feebly, yet does exist, and is always drawing more departments of economic life under its influence. Factory legislation, the democratising of local government . . . the freeing of trade unions . . . from legal restrictions . . . all these characterise this phase of the evolution. But the more the political organisations of modern nations are democratised the more the needs and opportunities of great political catastrophes are diminished.'

It is no great surprise, then, if for Bernstein socialism is, unproblematically, the continuation of liberalism,[34] and if, further, one of the ways in which he chooses to express this continuity is in terms of the harmony between means and ends: 'Democracy is at the same time means and end. It is the means of the struggle for socialism and it is the form socialism will take once it has been realised.'[35] It may be added here that Kautsky's polemic against the Bolsheviks in 1918 was nothing but an extended argument for this same proposition. Even then, after he had revealed himself in his true colours, Kautsky was not Bernstein. He did not transmute the socialist revolution into a cumulative process of reforms; he did still argue in terms of a proletarian conquest of power, of a 'political revolution . . . which is rapidly concluded.' But for him too the process had to remain within the framework of

[34] Bernstein, *op. cit.*, pp. xxv–xxvi, 148ff.
[35] Cited in P. Gay, *The Dilemma of Democratic Socialism,* New York 1962, pp. 244–5.

'democracy'. 'By the dictatorship of the proletariat', according to Kautsky, 'we are unable to understand anything else than its rule on the basis of democracy.'[36]

Now, of course, to show that something is true of Bernstein, or of Kautsky, does not by itself prove that it is false of Rosa Luxemburg. Indeed, did she not also tax the Bolsheviks in 1918 with the principle that democracy is an indispensable means in the creation of socialism? 'Socialist democracy', she then wrote, 'is not something which begins only in the promised land after the foundations of socialist economy are created . . . [it] begins simultaneously with the beginnings of the destruction of class rule and of the construction of socialism. It begins at the very moment of the seizure of power by the socialist party. It is the same thing as the dictatorship of the proletariat.'[37] But there is in fact a world of difference here. It has been a central concern of this book to elaborate on that difference, and the essential references have therefore been given to the sources in Luxemburg's work by which it can be substantiated. It would be superfluous to repeat them: as has already been shown, she clearly rejected the notion of a smooth continuity linking capitalism and socialism, whether in the guise of the idea of a gradual and progressive amelioration of capitalism's 'bad sides' in the context of perpetual peace and liberalism, or in that of an interclass conception of democracy and the state; she insisted that, in order to build socialism, the masses would have first to explode through that very framework of *bourgeois*-democratic institutions which both Bernstein and Kautsky wanted to preserve intact.[38] At this point we need only focus, then, on aspects of her thought that are especially relevant to our present theme.

Of first importance in this respect is her contention against Bernstein that the political democracy and juridical equality of bourgeois society are not inadequate expressions of

[36] K. Kautsky, *The Dictatorship of the Proletariat,* Ann Arbor 1964, pp. 56, 58, and cf. pp. 5, 42.

[37] 'The Russian Revolution', Waters, pp. 393–4.

[38] On this, see above pp. 35–6, 39–40, 51–7, 66, 115, 121–7.

socialism within capitalism, and thereby egalitarian forms in conflict with an inegalitarian social content, but wholly adequate expressions of capitalist economic relations which they serve both to legitimate and to protect. The contention is grounded in Luxemburg's grasp of Marx's political economy, a grasp that Bernstein could not match even in order to overturn the latter. In any case, where he posits an opposition between the legal/political and the economic orders of bourgeois society, between its liberal and democratic principle and the existing facts about class and inequality, which, however, as mere facts, are only contingent and transient, she by contrast identifies that kind of opposition as necessarily running the length and breadth of bourgeois society, through its economy and its polity and its law. It exists already within the economic relation: in the fact that by virtue of an exchange of equivalent economic values, of labour-power for the wage, the capitalist becomes enriched and the proletarian remains a proletarian, that is to say, impoverished relative to his own productive powers. 'Thus capitalist wealth', as Luxemburg herself puts it, 'is explained not... as the result of cheating or theft in the generally accepted sense of the words, but as an exchange between capitalist and worker, as a transaction of unimpeachable legal equity proceeding exactly according to those laws which govern the sale and purchase of all other commodities'.[39] For the legal forms which frame the economic relation embody a similar opposition. In what they say, there is nothing of class or exploitation, only an equality of rights between proprietors free to do business with one another. In what they allow however, amongst the time-honoured and, be it noted, *liberal* freedoms, by the freedom of property, there is the whole basis of exploitation: that the only productive asset of the vast majority of people, namely their own persons, is a source of need, while the property of a very few is a source, for them, of wealth, luxury and power. 'In our juridical system there

[39] 'The Second and Third Volumes [of *Capital*]', in F. Mehring, *Karl Marx*, London 1936, p. 372.

is not a single legal formula for the class domination of today', Luxemburg writes, and 'No law obliges the proletariat to submit itself to the yoke of capitalism. Poverty, the lack of means of production, obliges [it]'.[40] Finally, for Luxemburg the contradiction between democratic form and real class content lies at the interior of the state itself, and not between the state and civil society. In this once again she follows Marx, rather than one or another luminary of liberal-democratic thought, Marx who as early as the essay *On the Jewish Question* spoke of the *'sophistry of the political state'*,[41] intending to convey by this that the latter is not the instrument of human emancipation, that its claim to universality depends upon and does not dissolve the particularist conflicts of civil society, whose real dissolution therefore spells the death of this same state. She falls in, and not out, with the whole revolutionary Marxist tradition in regarding the state in capitalist society as precisely an 'instrumentality of oppression and class rule' (p. 102), which even in and through the democratic forms of universal citizenship assists in sanctioning the economic power of capital.

The political and juridical relations of bourgeois society are not then a seed of socialism. They are said by Luxemburg, in a rather different metaphor and for reasons to which we shall return, to constitute a 'wall' between capitalism and socialism, one which 'only the hammer blow of revolution, that is to say, *the conquest of political power by the proletariat can break down'*.[42] One can readily concede there to be some ambiguity in her occasional use, when discussing the bourgeois state, of the distinction between democratic form and class content. However, no great power of discrimination is needed to see that she was not thereby underwriting a continuity of political forms over the transition from capitalism to socialism. On the contrary, it comes out of every line of even that passage, from *Social Reform or Revolution,* which

[40] 'Social Reform or Revolution', Waters, pp. 78–9.
[41] T. B. Bottomore (ed.), *Karl Marx : Early Writings,* London 1963, p. 14.
[42] 'Social Reform or Revolution', Waters, p. 57.

Vollrath takes as his starting point, that she was concerned to dispute this very idea:

'On the one hand, we have the growth of the functions of a general interest on the part of the state, its intervention in social life, its "control" over society. But, on the other hand, its class character obliges the state to move the pivot of its activity and its means of coercion more and more into domains which are useful only to the class character of the bourgeoisie and have for society as a whole only a negative importance, as in the case of militarism and tariff and colonial policies. Moreover, the "social control" exercised by this state is at the same time penetrated with and dominated by its class character (see how labour legislation is applied in all countries). . . . The conflict within the capitalist state, described above, manifests itself even more emphatically in modern parliamentarism. Indeed, in accordance with its form, parliamentarism serves to express, within the organisation of the state, the interests of the whole of society. But what parliamentarism expresses here is capitalist society, that is to say, a society in which capitalist interests predominate. In this society, the representative institutions, democratic in form, are in content the instruments of the interests of the ruling class. This manifests itself in a tangible fashion in the fact that as soon as democracy shows the tendency to negate its class character and become transformed into an instrument of the real interests of the population, the democratic forms are sacrificed by the bourgeoisie and by its state representatives. That is why the idea of the conquest of a parliamentary reformist majority is a calculation which, entirely in the spirit of bourgeois liberalism, preoccupies itself only with one side – the formal side – of democracy, but does not take into account the other side, its real content. All in all, parliamentarism is not a directly socialist element impregnating gradually the whole capitalist society. It is, on the contrary, a specific form of the bourgeois class state, helping to ripen and develop the existing antagonisms of capitalism.'[43]

[43] *ibid.*, pp. 55–6; and cf. 'The Russian Revolution', Waters, p. 393.

For Rosa Luxemburg, the socialist revolution is neither the *incarnation* nor the *flowering* of a principle. It is a lengthy, epochal process of *struggle* to destroy exploitation and oppression and coercion, to release the productive powers of humankind and, by this, humankind itself from their subordination to the requirements of capital. As such, it cannot observe the kinds of harmony which the two analogies respectively suggest. It cannot pay homage only to its *telos*. In some measure, but, all the same, inevitably, it is also governed by the reality it undertakes to destroy. It is marked, *irredeemably*, by its beginning as well as by its end. Even to say that is an abstraction bordering on idealism, overlooking as it does, in the schematism of beginning and end, of capitalism and socialism, the multiple specificities of time and place which contribute their own exigencies far from the purity of pure socialism. Such specificities explain why, for example, the first act of this socialist revolution occurred when and where it did, in the most difficult circumstances conceivable. They do not, obviously, abolish the problem under discussion, the choice, for those who claim to oppose capitalism, between supporting the socialist revolution even with its 'impurities' – as Rosa Luxemburg supported that first difficult act, without a trace of cynical apologetics, with the frankest possible criticism, but on the basis of unflinching solidarity – and taking refuge in a moral purism that is in fact purely imaginary. Luxemburg herself pretended to no such purism, because she understood that painful and tragic historical dialectic in which, capitalism being both precondition and obstacle of socialism, the proletarian revolution could not escape from its violence in trying to rescue its achievements for the benefit of human beings. Since this revolution must count amongst its determinants at least these three moments – the resistance of capitalism, the achievements of capitalism, the project of human emancipation – it could correspond to the purity neither of the peaceful, organic transition nor of the clean break with the past. Espousing the ideal of humanity, Luxemburg did not dissolve within it the realities of class and of class power.

Indeed, her case against Bernstein explicitly covers his attempt at such a dissolution: 'The science, the democracy, the morality, considered by Bernstein as general, human, are merely the dominant science, dominant democracy and dominant morality, that is, bourgeois science, bourgeois democracy, bourgeois morality'. She takes him to task because he 'transforms socialism into a variety of liberalism' and thus 'deprives the socialist movement . . . of its class character', and because, under the notions of citizenship and 'man in general', 'he identifies . . . human society with bourgeois society'.[44] It is not that Rosa Luxemburg had no concern for humanity. The very opposite is true, and it is the more so because she coupled this humanitarian concern with a revolutionary realism rather than any assumption of universal goodwill. 'Ruthless revolutionary energy and tender humanity', she writes in 1918, 'this alone is the true essence of socialism. One world must now be destroyed, but each tear that might have been avoided is an indictment; and a man who hurrying on to important deeds inadvertently tramples underfoot even a poor worm is guilty of a crime.'[45] Later in the same year she repeats this humanitarian/realist couple but with its two terms reversed: 'The proletarian revolution does not need terror to realise its goals. It hates and abhors human murder.' So begins an argument in the programme of the Spartacus League, one which goes on to finish on the following note: 'The struggle for socialism is the mightiest civil war that world history has ever seen, and the proletarian revolution must prepare the necessary tools for this civil war, and must learn to use them – to fight and win.' The intermediate step in the argument is the 'life and death' struggle which 'all the beneficiaries and parasites of exploitation and class rule' are prepared to unleash against socialism: the 'savage desperation', the 'brutality, unconcealed cynicism, and baseness', the 'methods of cold malice . . . revealed throughout the history of colonialism', the 'massacres' and

[44] 'Social Reform or Revolution', Waters, pp. 85–6.
[45] 'A Duty of Honour', Looker, p. 261.

the 'methods of passive resistance', with which they will be ready to oppose it. This opposition must be met, according to Luxemburg, 'with an iron fist and unrelenting energy', the force of counter-revolution 'with the revolutionary force of the proletariat . . . with the arming of the people.'[46]

There are those who will no doubt be quick to see in this 'contradictory' couple just one link in a chain of reasoning that runs from Marx's notion of the dictatorship of the proletariat, or from Engels' characterisation of revolution quoted at the beginning of this section, to the labour camps and the purges of Stalinist Russia. To Marx and Engels it most certainly does connect, but what it connects to there is no disgrace to Marxism. It represents on the contrary one of Marxism's very finest traditions, namely, the aspiration to call things by their proper names, to tell it like it is, and the crimes of Stalin are separated from this tradition by a cacophony of lies. Luxemburg warns of the murderous resistance which the capitalist class, reacting to the revolutionary struggle for socialism as to a declaration of war, will try to mobilise to the defence of its interests under threat, and she exhorts the masses to be ready to defend themselves against it and to crush it. Without evincing in the slightest any tendency to extol or to glorify this necessity, she refrains from picturing it as an idyll of peace and libertarianism. She calls it what it is: a preparedness to use force, and armed force, in the struggle of the masses against their exploiters, a force which is not the less coercive of the latter for being a defence of the most vital interests of the former, their interest, in particular, in escaping from a paroxysm of blood-letting and repression. The clarity and the honesty of this position, the lack of either evasion or excess in its attitude towards the question of violence, these are a measure of Luxemburg's moral and political stature not merely against the grossly deformed shape of 'classical' Stalinism. It is a position that will easily bear comparison with the rhetoric of democratic and peaceful order employed typically by Social Democracy – the very same which its

[46] 'What Does the Spartakusbund Want?', Looker, pp. 279–81.

leading German representatives used at the moment of their complicity in the gangsterism that smashed Rosa Luxemburg's skull – whilst it continues, decade upon decade and at whatever cost, to support a *bourgeois order* that oppresses millions of people. It will bear comparison also with the statement, in one breath, both that socialism can be achieved 'by peaceful means and without armed struggle' and that the workers' movement 'will have the strength and the means to deal with the resistance of reaction *whatever form it may take'*: one way or another, an equivocal statement albeit unastonishingly so, coming as it does from *The British Road to Socialism,* pure concentrate of equivocation, since it wishes to give assurance, on its left, that its goal is the destruction of bourgeois society and, on its right, that it will play the game by bourgeois society's own rules.[47]

It is, however, facile to measure Luxemburg's stature in this regard against political traditions as corrupted as these are by apologetics on behalf of bureaucratic power. More interesting is a comparison with someone like Bookchin who has not this particular cross to bear. Yet Bookchin will do anything rather than squarely face the implications, destructive for libertarian purism, of the fact that the liberation of mankind does not already command universal agreement, that there are definite class interests and forms of power deployed against it. Here again the solvent qualities of that universal, humanity, are made to do their work in order to liquidate such inconvenient realities: '*A society based on self-administration must be achieved by means of self-administration* . . . power can only be destroyed by the very process in which *man* acquires power over his own life'.[48] Since what are brought into play, or rather conflict, here are on the one side power, and on the other just 'man', it may appear that the

---

[47] *The British Road to Socialism,* London 1968, p. 6, emphasis added; and cf. pp. 48–51. This equivocation is supported, predictably enough, by a certain vagueness on the question of 'democracy'. The programme, no less, of the *Communist* Party of Great Britain speaks a language in which 'democratic advance to socialism' is equated with 'winning political power without armed struggle' (p. 17), as though armed struggle were necessarily undemocratic.

[48] Bookchin, *op. cit.*, p. 167, second emphasis added.

ugly necessity of conflict between classes, and thus people, has been removed. It is, at any rate, a central theme of Bookchin's argument that the traditional classes are progressively decomposing to yield 'an entirely new "class" *whose very essence is that it is a non-class'*, 'entirely new subcultures which bear a resemblance to non-capitalist forms of relationships', 'a new human type . . . in ever-increasing numbers: the *revolutionary*'.[49] At the limit, this emergence of a new human being out of the decomposition of the traditional class structure seems to come close to corroding power, and the need for a struggle against it, out of existence. Hence: 'Discarding the tactical handbooks of the past, the revolution of the future follows the path of least resistance, eating its way into the most susceptible areas of the population irrespective of their "class position". . . . Here the form of the revolution becomes as total as its content – classless, propertyless, hierarchyless, and *wholly* liberating.'[50] Fine sentiment that! But just in case the sentiment is not enough, Bookchin lets us know, *twice* in a book of nearly three hundred pages, both times in passing, without pausing to reason out the consequences for his own libertarianism, that against the power of the bourgeois state and other incipient powers the people must be *armed,* and that armed confrontation between the people and the troops is something 'every revolution has to risk'.[51]

Does that not mean, anarchist, that violence may have to be done to create a society in which violence ceases, finally, to be done against people? And, on the side of the victims, will it be 'self-administered'? And can such violence be 'wholly' liberating? And, taking for granted that the answer to this last question must be negative since Bookchin will surely not want to enlist the services of that great commune in the sky, would it not be more honest to recognise that if revolution is indeed what is required, it cannot 'reflect' only the teleology of freedom? This matter is, after all, neither

[49] *ibid.*, pp. 185–6, 190.
[50] *ibid.*, pp. 191–2.
[51] *ibid.*, pp. 169, 267–8.

funny nor one where any old, arbitrarily chosen designation
will do. It is *deadly* serious. Just for this reason, no revolutionary should permit himself the kind of subterfuge by which
violence, revolutionary and counter-revolutionary, is tucked
away into a few casual lines whilst he pursues page after page
an edifying myth concerning the inseparability of process
and goal. In order to attain a somewhat less mythological
view, Bookchin could do worse than to take a harder look at
the tradition to which he proudly belongs. Through Paul
Avrich's book on Kronstadt, for example, he could remind
himself not only, as he does and is his right, of the broad,
populist language which the rebel sailors used by contrast
with what he calls the 'repressive jargon of Marxism';[52] but
also of their tough resistance, of the heavy, defensive barrage
of artillery and machine-gun fire which they threw out against
the Bolshevik forces attempting to take the fortress across the
precarious ice of the Gulf of Finland, a barrage which created
for these forces a truly fearsome, nightmarish and in no way
liberating experience and which left thousands of them dead.[53]
Even more to the point in a way, he could inform himself,
through another excellent book by the same historian, of the
quandary of the Russian anarchists during the civil war of
1918–1921, given their opposition to the notion of proletarian
dictatorship in general and to the Bolsheviks in particular,
but given also their obvious inability to countenance a White
victory; and of the fact that, their own ideological positions
and their criticisms of the Soviet government notwithstanding,
'a large majority' of them 'gave varying degrees of support' to
it. Some of them actually joined the Communist Party.[54]
Like Rosa Luxemburg, in other words, a majority of these
Russian anarchists adopted the only position possible in the
circumstances for real communists and socialists. No more
than she, did they thereby endorse everything the Bolsheviks
did or said. But did they not pay unwilling tribute, against
their own anti-authoritarian convictions and the temptations

[52] *ibid.*, pp. 244–5.
[53] P. Avrich, *Kronstadt 1921*, New York 1974, pp. 152–6, 202–12.
[54] P. Avrich, *The Russian Anarchists*, Princeton 1971, pp. 195–203.

of purism, to Engels, who forty-five years earlier maintained with exemplary clarity against another generation of anarchists that there is to the revolution an irreducibly authoritarian element? 'It is the act', he wrote, 'whereby one part of the population imposes its will upon the other part by means of rifles, bayonets and cannon – authoritarian means, if such there be at all.'[55]

In the article to which reference was made earlier, Anthony Arblaster mentions this view of Engels', and speaks of the growing number of socialists who would emphatically reject it and for whom 'if the revolution is authoritarian, it will have failed'.[56] However, if Arblaster counts himself amongst this number, as he seems to, he ought to address himself to answering Engels' specific contention rather than rejecting it on the basis of what are probably no more than the generalised and anachronistic imputations which the word, 'authoritarian', encourages. For Engels is perfectly specific about its meaning in this context. He is not talking about Gulag Archipelago, the political monopoly of 'the' party, or the unquestioned, and unquestionable, authority of the leader. He is talking of the need for the revolutionary forces to *impose* their will and to be ready and able to back this will with arms. That is the essence of the question and the question requires a straight answer. Can any revolution against capitalist wealth and power evade this necessity? If so, then one can be a libertarian but one must also be a pacifist. If not, then the revolution will fail unless it is authoritarian in the sense defined by Engels and to speak only of liberty in connection with it is tendentious.

From the historical references given no inference should be made, nor is it any part of this argument to suggest, that, in respect of the forms or the extent of violence, every socialist revolution must inevitably be modelled on the Russian, or that no such revolution can be complete without some given quota of bloodshed, or even that there is some revolutionary principle which requires that violence be done. It should not

[55] 'On Authority', *loc. cit.*
[56] 'The Relevance of Anarchism', *loc. cit.*, p. 170.

be necessary to make these points explicitly, but it is, for the benefit of people quick to fall into this type of misunderstanding: both those who declare themselves simply 'against' violence or 'against' authority (as if Marxist revolutionaries could be 'in favour of' either the one or the other), and those who commit themselves to peace at least here, where the 'democratic' tradition is strong, and now that times have changed. There are good reasons, in any case, to hope that the labour movements of the advanced capitalist countries will not have to repeat the bitter experience of the Russian proletariat. They are immeasurably stronger, both numerically and politically, than it was. Actually or potentially, they have at their command cultural, economic and technical resources that are incomparably greater. They are in a position also to take advantage of its experience as well as other subsequent experiences, and of not having to make the *first* attempt to sustain proletarian rule in a completely hostile environment. However, all of the advantages they enjoy are a consequence of various types of strength, not weakness, and it is no different in the matter under discussion. The prospect for any working class movement, once embarked upon a serious struggle for socialism, of escaping from prolonged or massive violence, will be maximised precisely in the measure that it is equipped, both ideologically and materially, to move with resolution against any counter-revolutionary resistance and to stamp it out. Simply to count in advance on there being no serious resistance is to disarm the workers' movement ideologically, and in the event materially as well, by sowing illusions. Today, knowing what we do about the hideous repression which ruling classes in danger are willing to unleash against the masses, about the widespread practice of brutal torture, about fascist mass movements, the activities of 'intelligence' agencies, the overt and the covert forms of foreign intervention, and so on *ad nauseam,* it is obligatory to *expect* serious resistance and an act of the grossest folly and negligence to pretend to speak in earnest about revolution whilst simultaneously identifying that process only with peace or liberty. From every point of view, therefore, it is wrong to elide the revolution's *coercive* dimension: its programme of taking by force what is held in the last instance by force – of taking the wealth of the capitalist class, its *freedom* to exploit and to dominate working people, many other *freedoms* which it alone enjoys and are based upon this one – and of being prepared to suppress any violent reaction against this expropriation. In that sense, what Engels wrote a century ago remains true to this day.

At the same time, it must not be overlooked that he was speaking only of one dimension of revolution and not offering an overall characterisation. What he wrote is no vindication of the claim that, in some standard Marxist view, 'revolution is a means to an end that is altogether different from revolution',[57] force and nothing but force, as it were, to win the realm of freedom. Engels' words on the authoritarian character of revolution are as compatible as Marx's on the dictatorial character of proletarian rule with the view that the proletarian revolution, as an act of self-emancipation, must create for the masses forms of democracy and of freedom that are more real, more effective and more extensive than any they have enjoyed hitherto. For the record, it should also be pointed out here that the words of Karl Korsch quoted alongside those of Engels at the beginning of this section, and emphasising precisely this dimension of freedom, are not, despite possible appearances to the contrary, despite the ambiguity of prefiguration which they too contain, a repudiation on his part of the dictatorship of the proletariat. On the contrary, Korsch situates them explicitly within a recognition of its necessity. Engels on authority and Korsch on freedom, these are not two different positions, the one authoritarian, the other libertarian. They are two sides of one position: revolutionary Marxist. And that position, *both* sides of it, is the position also of Rosa Luxemburg:

'Yes, dictatorship! But this dictatorship consists in the *manner of applying democracy,* not in its *elimination,* in energetic, resolute attacks upon the well-entrenched rights and

[57] See above p. 140.

economic relationships of bourgeois society, without which a socialist transformation cannot be accomplished.'

'The proletariat, when it seizes power, . . . must at once undertake socialist measures in the most energetic, unyielding and unhesitant fashion, in other words, exercise a dictatorship, but a dictatorship of the *class,* not of a party or of a clique – dictatorship of the class, that means in the broadest public form on the basis of the most active, unlimited participation of the mass of the people, of unlimited democracy.'

'Revolutionary idealism . . . can be maintained over any length of time only through the intensively active life of the masses themselves under conditions of unlimited political freedom.'

'It is a well-known and indisputable fact that without a free and untrammelled press, without the unlimited right of association and assemblage, the rule of the broad mass of the people is entirely unthinkable.'[58]

All of these passages are from Luxemburg's pamphlet, *The Russian Revolution,* and to take from them only *one* side of her position, to transform her, on the pretext of some phrases concerning freedom and democracy, into another political creature, be it a liberal, so-called 'democratic socialist' (i.e. Social-Democrat in the contemporary sense of that word), or libertarian – that is a useless game. As if either liberalism or 'democratic socialism' so defined anywhere, ever, stood for a determined assault against the economic rights and relationships of bourgeois society through the kind of prodigious mass activity to which she here alludes; and as if they stood for a freedom or democracy for the masses that was anything like unlimited. As if libertarianism could acknowledge so frankly and unequivocally, without thereby removing its own basis, that the destruction of bourgeois society necessarily involves the proletariat in the seizure and the use of power.

In the end we have returned to our beginning, to the

[58] 'The Russian Revolution', Waters, pp. 394, 393, 392, 389.

reflections on democratic freedom in Luxemburg's criticism of the Bolsheviks in 1918, actual, historical point of departure for more than one attempt to denature the sense of her work. To deal with them was our end from the beginning, this being an indispensable part of the more general exercise of trying to recuperate that sense in its integrity. By means of the foregoing encounter with ideas that impede and retard this effort of recovery, we have reached a position where her pamphlet on the Russian revolution can be treated directly on its own terrain, that of revolutionary Marxism. Here too, however, even upon that terrain, similar impediments to a proper understanding of her meaning are to be found. Indeed, as early as the beginning of 1922, in the first serious critique of the pamphlet by a Marxist, Georg Lukacs identified as the faults basic to Luxemburg's arguments concerning democracy her tendency to 'oppose to the exigencies of the moment the principles of future stages of the revolution' and her 'overestimation of *the organic character* of the course of history'. There is an evident symmetry between this double attribution and the twofold, spiritual-and-organic relation of means to ends, stipulated by both reformism and libertarianism in order to liquidate, respectively, the future into the present and the present into the future. Lukacs was far from wanting to anathematise Rosa Luxemburg, speaking of her here as 'the unforgettable teacher and leader of revolutionary Marxism'.[59] Having himself, only the year before, devoted an essay to the power and the originality of her Marxism,[60] he ventured no suggestion of either reformism or anarchism in her thought. At the end of 1922, in the preface to the celebrated collection of essays in which these two appeared, he still wrote that 'a truly revolutionary, Communist and Marxist position can be acquired only through a critical confrontation with the theoretical life's work of Rosa Luxemburg',[61] an opinion not very different from Lenin's of the same year. Lukacs' criticisms of her pamphlet, then, were

[59] G. Lukacs, *History and Class Consciousness,* London 1971, pp. 276–7.
[60] *ibid.*, pp. 27–45.
[61] *ibid.*, p. xlii.

directed at what he saw as errors, but as the errors of an outstanding revolutionary within a framework squarely Marxist.

Nevertheless, the particular criticisms cited are grounded in a reading of Luxemburg's text which is disputable, and in proffering them Lukacs contributed, in the company once again of Lenin himself,[62] to initiating a long and still going tradition within revolutionary Marxism of regarding that text as simply another in an ample list of her 'mistakes'. *The Russian Revolution* is not free from mistakes: at least one of them Luxemburg herself subsequently recognised as such; another of them she had sustained throughout her political life and merely repeated here in saying that 'the famous "right of self-determination of nations" is nothing but hollow, petty-bourgeois phraseology and humbug'.[63] Yet in view of the historical sequel it is today implausible to see the preoccupations of the pamphlet as just mistaken, and unilateral to overlook its considerable merits. Not the least important thing about it is the fact that a work of this kind was written at all at the time: in 1918, under the full impact of the encouragement and inspiration which revolutionaries everywhere drew from the example of the first successful proletarian revolution, a work quite empty of any reverence, combining an independent, critical spirit with the most wholehearted sympathy and support. 'Whatever a party could offer of courage, revolutionary far-sightedness and consistency in a historic hour, Lenin, Trotsky and the other comrades have given in good measure. All the revolutionary honour and capacity which western Social Democracy lacked were represented by the Bolsheviks. Their October uprising was not only the actual salvation of the Russian revolution; it was also the salvation of the honour of international socialism.'[64] These are not the words of someone of doubtful or vacillating loyalties. They are lavish praise. Luxemburg, however, had

---

[62] On this opinion of Lenin's, see *Collected Works*, Vol. 33, p. 210, and above p. 130.

[63] 'The Russian Revolution', Waters, p. 379.

[64] *ibid.*, p. 375; and cf. pp. 394–5.

no hesitation in qualifying praise with criticism, considering it to be axiomatic that, in the difficult conditions in which this revolution was being made, it was bound to exhibit features of which socialists must take a critical view. They should not defer to the 'spotless authority' of the Russian example.[65] It has, of course, become something of a cliché of revolutionary writing to stress the virtues of criticism and self-criticism, as she did many times, designating them on one occasion 'life and breath for the proletarian movement'.[66] Cliché though it may be, in 1918 she was not content to voice it. She practised it, and that practice then, in relation to its particular object, and by a Marxist revolutionary, was in no way stereotypical. Unwilling to be overawed by the first proletarian conquest of power, she marched out her criticisms one by one, mistakes and all. Doing so, she displayed towards the immensely enhanced moral authority of Bolshevism and of Lenin a strength, an independence of judgment, the courage and the capacity to uphold, in relative isolation, principled positions which she thought to be right. That in itself is a fact not to be belittled in view of the crippling epigonism which soon came to surround Lenin's name and all his works.

As to the substance of the pamphlet's arguments on democracy, it is necessary in the first place to be clear about what they were. Even Lukacs who held Luxemburg's work in high regard shows a certain lack of care in the way he handles them. On the one hand, he himself draws attention to the fact that she did not here forswear or condemn the use of revolutionary violence, that she stated explicitly that socialism 'has as its pre-requisite a number of measures of force – against property, etc.' He says also, quite rightly, that she was not concerned 'to offer a . . . defence of democracy "in general"'.[67] On the other hand, however, he is led to flatly contradict what he thus knows to be the case, and that by his claim, noted above, and nowhere substantiated in detail, that her arguments on democracy are based upon her

[65] *ibid.*, pp. 368–9.
[66] 'The Junius Pamphlet', Waters, p. 262.
[67] Lukacs, *op. cit.*, pp. 277, 290; and 'The Russian Revolution', Waters, p. 390.

practice of counterposing to the exigencies of the present the principles of the future. For the only points relevant to this claim, points which might begin to make some sense of it, occur when Lukacs concludes his treatment of the topic by saying, as if in opposition to Luxemburg, 'Freedom cannot represent a value in itself. . . . *Freedom must serve the rule of the proletariat, not the other way round*'; and when he starts it by speaking of her emphatic disapproval of the denial of rights to the bourgeoisie on the part of the Bolsheviks.[68] But in the light of these imputations it is no longer clear why her defence of democracy is not a defence of democracy 'in general', in the manner of Kautsky and the manner that would oppose her, as so many have tried to oppose her, to the proletariat's *dictatorship* over its class enemies. It could of course be that the contradiction is in Luxemburg, as Lukacs probably wished to suggest, rather than in Lukacs himself. It could be, but is not, as can be seen from the following passage, limpid in its distinction from either liberalism or libertarianism, a passage to which Lukacs makes no reference and to which, indeed, reference is very rarely made:

'As the entire middle class, the bourgeois and petty-bourgeois intelligentsia, boycotted the Soviet government for months after the October Revolution and crippled the railroad, post and telegraph, and educational and administrative apparatus, and, in this fashion, opposed the workers' government, naturally enough all measures of pressure were exerted against it. These included the deprivation of political rights, of economic means of existence, etc., in order to break their resistance with an iron fist. It was precisely in this way that the socialist dictatorship expressed itself, for it cannot shrink from any use of force to secure or prevent certain measures involving the interests of the whole.'[69]

What Lukacs imputes to Luxemburg, in other words, is the

[68] Lukacs, pp. 292, 277.
[69] 'The Russian Revolution', Waters, p. 388.

very opposite of what she says here and it is not founded by him on anything else she says. Her concern about freedom is manifestly over its scope within the dictatorship of the proletariat rather than over a principle above the dictatorship of the proletariat. It is a concern for the most extensive, thoroughgoing and 'unlimited' democratic rights and liberties compatible with proletarian rule and, to that extent, it satisfies the criterion stipulated by Lukacs himself. This does not exhaust the matter for what she and he understand by that general stipulation is not the same. We shall return to the point, however, after examining the other attribution which he makes to her.

This is, as was indicated, an overestimation of the 'organic' character of the historical process. Here again, Lukacs knows Luxemburg's work too well to saddle her firmly and unambiguously with that. He himself points to some of the evidence against it, to sources in her work where she shows 'that the idea of an organic "growth" into socialism is untenable', and he even credits her with being 'one of the first people to advance the opposite view'.[70] In the face of this evidence, however, he not only persists with his ascription but, going further, complements it with another, namely, that '*she imagines the proletarian revolution as having the structural forms of bourgeois revolutions*'. Now, no reader of Luxemburg's writings, not even one completely hardened in a conviction of her economism and spontaneism, will be able seriously to sustain the view that she sees the transition to socialism as a largely *unconscious* process in which a socio-economic revolution is accomplished *before* any fundamental political transformation occurs. But this is just what Lukacs wants to ascribe to her by invoking the parallel with bourgeois revolutions. According to him, she is supposed to have thought that 'the proletarian state . . . can only arise as an ideological "superstructure" *after and in consequence of* a socio-economic revolution that has *already taken place*'; and, in line with this thought, to have failed to note the active role of class conscious-

---

[70] Lukacs, pp. 277–9; and cf. above n. 38 of this essay and text.

ness in the socialist transformation 'in contrast to the *post festum* recognitions of the bourgeoisie'. Because it gives priority to an unconscious and thus automatic economic transition to socialism, this thought is obviously coherent with the claim that Luxemburg overestimates the organic character of the process. But it is not Luxemburg's thought. Indeed, in these few pages of *History and Class Consciousness,* there is a truly strange, and, to the best of our knowledge, hitherto unremarked upon spectacle: in one voice Lukacs takes her to task for ideas which he concedes in another voice not to have been hers, and he deploys against her arguments so strikingly similar in form and content to her own, that the likelihood is he must have learned them from her. Such for example are the arguments: 'The natural laws of capitalism do indeed lead inevitably to its ultimate crisis but at the end of *its* road would be the destruction of all civilisation and a new barbarism'; and 'Even the most highly developed capitalist concentration will still be qualitatively different, even economically, from a socialist system and can neither change into one "by itself" nor will it be amenable to such change "through legal devices" within the framework of capitalist society'.[71] At the bottom of this surreal spectacle is, once again, Lukacs' somewhat free and easy way with what Luxemburg writes.

At least here, however, in the case of the organic transition, he tries to marshal some evidence for his claim rather than simply making an unsupported imputation. The evidence consists of two arguments from *The Russian Revolution.* One of them need not detain us for more than a moment since Lukacs simply misunderstands it and it supports nothing he wants to say. In one section of the pamphlet, Luxemburg expresses a concern lest the right of suffrage devised by the

[71] Lukacs, pp. 280–4. For Luxemburg's express rejection of the idea that the proletarian revolution has 'the structural forms of bourgeois revolutions', see 'Speech to the Hanover Congress (1899)', D. Howard (ed.), *Selected Political Writings of Rosa Luxemburg,* New York and London 1971, pp. 44–6; on the 'ultimate crisis' and 'barbarism', see above pp. 13–42; on capitalist concentration and change 'through legal devices', see 'Social Reform or Revolution', Waters, pp. 78–80.

Soviet government and based upon 'a general obligation to labour' will have the effect of disenfranchising not only 'the exploiters', as is its intention, but also 'broad and growing sections of the petty bourgeoisie and proletariat for whom the economic mechanism provides no means of exercising the obligation to work'. The point she makes is that, in the prevailing conditions of great economic dislocation and chaos, such a suffrage law is inappropriate because many who want to work are unable to. In *this* context she speaks of it as an 'anachronism' which anticipates an economic position that does not yet exist.[72] The point is quite precise and limited. But by abstracting a few lines from the context so that this specific point disappears altogether, Lukacs takes Luxemburg to be offering a general hypothesis on the transition to socialism, to the effect that the proletarian state and law can only sanction *post facto* what has been 'brought about by economic forces beyond the control of consciousness'.[73] That mistake bears the whole responsibility for the comparison with bourgeois revolutions. The other of Luxemburg's arguments which he brings forward as evidence appears superficially to prove his case. It is worth quoting for it leads us to the central issue:

'The socialist system of society should only be, and can only be, a historical product, born out of the school of its own experiences, born in the course of its realisation, as a result of the developments of living history, which – just like organic nature of which, in the last analysis, it forms a part – has the fine habit of always producing along with any real social need the means to its satisfaction, along with the task simultaneously the solution. However, if such is the case, then it is clear that socialism by its very nature cannot be decreed or introduced by *ukase*.'[74]

There is here not only the explicit parallel with organic

---

[72] 'The Russian Revolution', Waters, pp. 387–9.

[73] Lukacs, p. 280.

[74] 'The Russian Revolution', Waters, p. 390.

nature but also the overt spontaneism of the notion that the
solution is 'always' produced contemporaneously with the
task. Against this, one could point out that that notion is a
clear allusion to the classics, indeed to what could be called
the classic of historical materialism, namely Marx's 'Preface'
to *A Contribution to the Critique of Political Economy*,[75] and
that not too much can be made of the combination of such a
passing allusion with a brief, parenthetical simile. But there
is no need to rely on any special plea of this kind. Readers may
decide for themselves what is the proper weight to be attached
to the evidence of these lines. The most important point, and
one not irrelevant to that decision, is the substance of what
Luxemburg is saying in the pages from which this evidence
has been mined.

Even in the above lines, which are the ones Lukacs himself
cites, traces of this substance have been left. For the meaning
of the argument that socialism, maturing in the school of its
experiences, cannot be decreed into life, is the very opposite
of the one he wishes to give it. It is not the statement of a
conviction in the automatic and unconscious nature of the
socialist revolutionary process, nor an appeal to the self-
sufficiency of blind, economic forces, one such as must dis-
parage the importance of conscious, political struggle and of
the efforts and the legal enactments of the proletarian state.
It is scarcely credible that Lukacs could so badly misunder-
stand Luxemburg's meaning. She is appealing, in any case,
to a rather different distinction: between a socialism which is
commanded into existence by bureaucratic fiat, and a socialism – in reality the only possible kind – which is won by the
masses through a prodigious effort of struggle, through
victories and defeats, through errors, misjudgments, but also
new political and intellectual acquisitions; a socialism that
establishes their conscious and collective control over the
whole of the social process and, as such, cannot be achieved
through an unconscious or automatic development, behind
their backs as it were, to be ratified only subsequently by an

[75] Marx and Engels, *Selected Works*, Vol. 1, p. 504.

act of recognition and some necessary superstructural adjust-
ments. How little this conception resembles one of an organic
or spontaneous transition is plain from virtually everything
Luxemburg says both immediately before and immediately
after the quoted passage. It is in these pages that she speaks
of the political education of the masses as the indispensable
basis of proletarian rule, and of the 'intensive political training'
needed to match the 'giant tasks' undertaken by the Bolsheviks.
It is here too that freedom is said to be ineffective when it
becomes a special privilege, and given a situation where it is
necessary 'step by step . . . to feel out the ground, try out,
experiment, test now one way now another'. There are some
signposts, she says, but no ready formulas to the socialist
transformation, no easy key to the 'thousand concrete,
practical measures, large and small' that are required. 'New
territory. A thousand problems. Only experience is capable
of correcting and opening new ways.' Only by their energetic
participation in political and social life will it be possible to
achieve 'a complete spiritual transformation in the masses. . . .
Social instincts in place of egotistical ones, mass initiative in
place of inertia, idealism which conquers all suffering, etc,
etc.'[76] With its emphasis on the inevitably tentative, experimental, even mistaken, character of a great deal of revolutionary effort and on the untiring battle needed in turn to
adjust and correct its results, all of this perhaps helps to
provide some perspective on the notion that the task 'simultaneously' finds its solution, a notion significant if at all only
in an epochal sense.

Criticism and self-criticism, these are no mere cliché, nor
even only some abstract ethical requirement. They are
definitive of the character of the proletarian revolution and
turn out thereby to be the crux of the matter. Writ large in
these pages from *The Russian Revolution,* they secrete another
allusion to the classics, and that a surer guide to Luxemburg's
thought than the one which caught Lukacs' attention. In

[76] 'The Russian Revolution', Waters, pp. 389–91; cf. above text for n. 3 and
n. 11 of this essay.

The Eighteenth Brumaire of Louis Bonaparte Marx wrote:

'Proletarian revolutions . . . criticise themselves constantly, interrupt themselves continually in their own course, come back to the apparently accomplished in order to begin it afresh, deride with unmerciful thoroughness the inadequacies, weaknesses and paltrinesses of their first attempts, seem to throw down their adversary only in order that he may draw new strength from the earth and rise again, more gigantic, before them, recoil ever and anon from the indefinite prodigiousness of their own aims, until a situation has been created which makes all turning back impossible, and the conditions themselves cry out:

> *Hic Rhodus, hic salta!*
> *Here is the rose, here dance!'*[77]

Luxemburg makes no explicit reference to this passage here, though on other occasions she did.[78] However, the model it contains, not of the *simultaneity* of revolutionary task and solution, but of the inherent *prematurity* by which every proletarian revolution is afflicted, is one which she had firmly integrated into her thinking as early as the revisionist controversy. As Lukacs himself understood, it is the very antithesis of an 'organic' conception and he even recognised its presence in this pamphlet.[79] All he failed to recognise was its presence in the very lines adduced by him as the site of Luxemburg's errors.

Why then prematurity? It is not only because the Bolsheviks were the first with this endeavour, nor merely because of the acutely difficult circumstances they faced, that she spoke of the unavoidably tentative character of all they did. She was explicit to the contrary: 'Thus it must and will be with all of us when we get to the same point.'[80] Further, it is only a

[77] Marx and Engels, *Selected Works,* Vol. 1, p. 401.

[78] See 'Social Reform or Revolution', Waters, p. 89, and 'Rebuilding the International', Looker, p. 205.

[79] Lukacs, pp. 278–9; see above pp. 51–2.

[80] 'The Russian Revolution', Waters, p. 390.

rough approximation to say, following her own indications and, before hers, Marx's, that it is owing to the *immensity* of the tasks and the obstacles that no proletarian revolution can be so adequately prepared from the beginning as to be able to find ready solutions. The deeper meaning of this notion is that between the historical point of departure of the capitalist economy and polity, and the nature of the socialist objective, there is a specific *qualitative* difference which makes it impossible for solutions to be given in advance and unavoidable that they be sought and won by long exertion. That qualitative difference was defined in one of Luxemburg's economic texts when she referred to the situation where 'the anarchistic economy of capitalism has made way for a planful, organised economic order which will be systematically directed and managed by the entire working force of mankind'.[81] The thought was not especially novel even then, but it embodies a lot of what matters in this context: in particular, the distinction between an economy which is opaque to the masses and beyond their control, and one which they both understand and manage. Congruent with this distinction, resting upon and reinforcing it, is another: between a democracy which restricts their political activity within very narrow limits and excludes them from both active participation in, and a rational consciousness of, the processes of public administration; and a democracy which bursts those limits to admit them to the one and to the other. The transition to socialism is an attempt to cross the gulf of this distinction. That is the *fundamental* reason why any 'organic' conception of it has to be rejected. The questions of the extent of counter-revolutionary and revolutionary violence, and of whether or not the capitalist class is to be deprived of the vote, are in this sense secondary, matters of circumstance, probability or possibility, rather than of principle. But the necessity to destroy economic relations in which the labouring populace is exploited and mystified and political institutions which all but exclude it from politics, this is integral to the

[81] 'What is Economics?', Waters, p. 245.

objective. Socialism cannot be given as the end product of an organic development of objective economic laws since it presupposes the abolition of those laws and their wretched objectivity. It cannot be given as the end product of an organic process of cumulative improvements within the framework of bourgeois-democratic institutions since it presupposes the demolition of that framework. The revolution has to destroy, to break up, to shatter a whole elaborate institutional structure which expropriates the masses economically and politically. And it has to release all their creative energies into a work which is, at last, their own: thus – unprecedentedly – to build through their own organisations, their own parties, councils and assemblies, their own newspapers, and with their own voice, a society that is fit for human beings. Except by way of general guidelines, therefore, socialism can also not be given in a programme or a theory; nor can it be given by the legislative and administrative dictates of the guardians of some orthodoxy. Simply, it cannot be *given*. It has to be won by and of the effort of working people for the needs of working people. It is a break with one world towards another, a break which, it is now surely needless to argue, cannot be clean or punctual, because it will always be premature however overdue. Rosa Luxemburg during the German revolution, once, again, and yet again: socialism cannot be introduced by decree. Because it is an organic-economic or spontaneous process beyond the reach of political initiative? Nothing of the kind. Because it must be politically fought for and politically won by 'the conscious will and action of the majority of the proletariat'.[82]

There remain, out of this whole aspect of Lukacs' criticisms, two things, one big and one small. The small thing is Luxemburg's reprimand of the Bolsheviks over the dissolution of the Constituent Assembly in January 1918. To appreciate that such is its significance one must situate it historically. Imprisoned, and thus cut off from adequate sources of

---

[82] 'The Beginning', 'The National Assembly' and 'What Does the Spartakusbund Want?', Looker, pp. 253, 265, 277; 'Speech to the Founding Convention of the German Communist Party', Waters, p. 419.

information, she did no more than respond to what she understood to be the justification of that act offered by the Bolsheviks themselves. Now, there were in this justification two distinct strands. The basic one was that the Constituent Assembly was a bourgeois parliament become the rallying point for the gathering forces of counter-revolution, and hence doubly opposed to the soviets which, as organs of workers' democracy, expressed the proletarian-socialist charater of the October Revolution, and had every right to supersede that parliament. The second strand was that owing to a number of contingent circumstances (split within the SRs, timing of the elections, etc.) the composition of the Assembly did not adequately reflect the actual, current relation of forces in the country. Seizing only on this second argument in isolation from the first, Luxemburg simply overlooked the point that the dissolution of the Assembly was done in the interest of proletarian democracy, and thought that she detected here revolutionary impatience with any kind of democratic 'formalities'. If the composition of this body did not properly reflect the present state of affairs then why not, she asked, arrange new elections? She saw its dissolution, in other words, as one manifestation of a certain carelessness towards democratic rights in general on the part of the Bolsheviks under pressure, rather than as the liquidation of a bourgeois-democratic institution by and for a democracy of the masses.[83] We have argued that Rosa Luxemburg went further than her contemporaries before 1917 in anticipating the nature of proletarian power.[84] But in view of the fact that the question of its precise institutional forms remained an open one in the absence of any successful proletarian revolution, and of the ambiguity in the Bolshevik position even in

[83] 'The Russian Revolution', Waters, pp. 384–7. The arguments of Trotsky with which Luxemburg here takes issue, and which focus on the composition of the Constituent Assembly, are from 'The History of the Russian Revolution to Brest-Litovsk', in *The Essential Trotsky,* London 1963, pp. 91–5. On this question, see also E. H. Carr, *The Bolshevik Revolution 1917–23,* 3 vols., Harmondsworth 1966, Vol. 1, pp. 119–29; and M. Liebman, *Leninism Under Lenin,* London 1975, pp. 232–8.

[84] See above pp. 121–5.

1917, calling for '*All* power to the soviets!' *and* the convocation of the Constituent Assembly up to the very seizure of power; in view of Luxemburg's incarceration at this time which prevented her from making a well-informed assessment, and of her recognition, when she was in a position to do so, shortly after her release, during the course of the German revolution, that her criticism in this matter had been mistaken[85] – in view of all this it is neither surprising that she was able to make this mistake nor possible to attach great significance to it where the interpretation of her thought is concerned. To treat it, as Lukacs does, in the context of his criticisms discussed above, as flowing logically from her whole conception of proletarian revolution is to make an arbitrary connection. After all, only a couple of months later she could declare in no uncertain terms that this type of assembly was a bourgeois institution counterposed to the organs of workers' democracy and a 'counter-revolutionary stronghold' against them,[86] without for all that ceasing to subscribe to the substantive views expressed in *The Russian Revolution* and summed up in the assertion that socialism cannot be 'decreed'. The long passage below, which follows and elaborates one such assertion, shows clearly enough these same views in comfortable coexistence with the correction of the mistake in question.

'The mass of the proletariat is called upon not merely to define the aims and direction of the revolution with clear understanding. It must itself, through its own activity, nurse socialism, step by step, to life. The essence of socialist society is that the great working mass ceases to be a ruled mass and instead lives and controls its own political and economic life in conscious and free self-determination. Thus from the highest offices of the state down to the smallest municipality, the proletarian mass must replace the outdated organs of

---

[85] Cf. J. P. Nettl, *Rosa Luxemburg*, 2 vols., London 1966, Vol. 2, pp. 700, 703, 718, where this is conceded rather grudgingly.

[86] 'The National Assembly' and 'The Elections to the National Assembly', Looker, pp. 262–5, 287–90.

bourgeois class rule – the federal councils, parliaments, municipal councils – with their own class organs: the workers' and soldiers' councils. Further, the proletarian mass must fill all posts, supervise all functions and measure all the state's requirements against their own class interests and against the tasks of socialism. And only in a constant, active interrelation between the masses and their organs, the workers' and soldiers' councils, can the masses' activity fill the state with the socialist spirit. . . . In tenacious hand-to-hand struggle against capitalism in every firm and factory, through the direct pressure of the masses and through strikes, and by creating their own representative organs, the workers can gain control over production and ultimately the actual leadership. . . . All . . . socialist civic virtues, together with the knowledge and ability to manage socialist operations, can be acquired by the working class only through their own activity, their own experience. . . . The socialisation of society can be realised only by the stubborn and untiring struggle of the working class on all fronts. . . . The liberation of the working class must be the work of the working class itself.'[87]

This last sentiment returns us, conveniently, to the major issue still outstanding, namely, the scope of democratic rights and liberties within the dictatorship of the proletariat. In its general lines, Luxemburg's view on the issue is clear. The proletarian dictatorship is a more direct and more extensive form of democracy than anything that has existed hitherto and must involve comprehensive democratic procedures and freedoms: elections, freedom of the press, freedom of opinion – for the one who thinks differently, not only for the members of one party – freedom of assembly, etc., in the absence of which 'life dies out in every public institution, becomes a mere semblance of life, in which only the bureaucracy remains as the active element . . . an elite of the working class is invited from time to time to meetings where they are to applaud the speeches of the leaders, and to approve

[87] 'What Does the Spartakusbund Want?', Looker, pp. 277–8.

proposed resolutions unanimously'.[88] Her view demands *freedom in other words for a plurality of tendencies and parties within the dictatorship of the proletariat.* In this connection, Lukacs speaks disparagingly of the distinction she makes between dictatorship of the party and of the class, and also of her dangerous proximity 'to exaggerating utopian expectations and to anticipating later phases in the process'.[89] One should be clear, therefore, about a couple of points. Luxemburg did not begrudge or question the Bolsheviks' title to hegemony in Russia, stating categorically that they were the *only* party that had grasped the true nature and needs of the situation in 1917 and won thereby support, leadership and power.[90] So we are not dealing here with yet further evidence of her notorious 'spontaneism'. We are dealing with a concern lest, by the elimination of the possibilities of opposition and criticism, the proletarian state should come to be automatically identified with the Bolshevik party and the interests of the working masses with the will of a bureaucratic leadership. Secondly, it is idle to represent this concern as nothing more than a purist flaunting of principle in defiance of the exigencies of the moment. For, she was again perfectly explicit in saying that what the Bolsheviks had done in this direction was 'forced upon them' by circumstances in which it was impossible and unreasonable to expect from them the finest example of socialist democracy. What she did insist on, however, and this is ultimately the crucial merit of her pamphlet, was that in coping with these temporary exigencies the temptation should be avoided of taking them for general principles, and thus making 'a virtue of necessity'.[91] That is the grain of 'truth', if one wants, in the charge of utopianism, but it is hardly to be accounted a weakness in her positions. The surest demonstration that it is, on the contrary, a strength is given by what Lukacs himself in 1922 opposed to the Luxemburg

[88] 'The Russian Revolution', Waters, p. 391.
[89] Lukacs, p. 291.
[90] 'The Russian Revolution', Waters, pp. 372, 374.
[91] *ibid.*, pp. 394–5.

of 1918 on the subject of freedom and the proletarian dictatorship.

He had no quarrel with the notion that the possibility of criticism 'must be kept open institutionally even under the dictatorship'. But against the idea that such institutional openness required the existence of certain specific political rights and liberties, he proposed a rather different answer. The proletarian dictatorship, he argued, is a period of abrupt changes in the state of the class struggle, in which the proletariat must be able to manoeuvre and make quick turns, whether on economic policy or on the extent of freedom. Against this background: 'Only a revolutionary party like that of the Bolsheviks is able to carry out these often very sudden changes of front. Only such a party is sufficiently adaptable, flexible and independent in judgment of the actual forces at work to be able to advance from Brest-Litovsk and the war-communism of the fiercest civil wars to the new economic policy. Only the Bolsheviks will be able to progress from that policy (in the event of new shifts in the balance of power) to yet other power-groupings while preserving unimpaired the essential dominance of the proletariat'. By contrast, according to Lukacs, all other tendencies in the workers' movement are counter-revolutionary and there is a straight line 'from Kornilov to Kronstadt'.[92] The answer, in essence, is simple: the party knows. The 'spotless authority' of the Russian example has, here, already done its work.

We have refrained in this book, and will do so to the end, from any attempt to assess the global political and strategic conceptions of Rosa Luxemburg by means of a systematic comparison with those of Lenin. Reference has been made to him in passing and there was a sustained comparison between his and her perspectives on the Russian revolution after 1905. But there it was a question of drawing attention to a fundamental unanimity. The procedure, which is so common, of discussing problems such as those of spontaniety and consciousness, organisation and the mass struggle, and so on, by

[92] Lukacs, pp. 292–3.

continual reference to her points of difference with the Leninist theory of them, has been deliberately eschewed. For, the procedure is methodologically unsound and produces inevitable distortions in the interpretation of her work. If the principle of intelligibility of her thought is not wholly internal, extending beyond her texts into the broader politico-ideological field which was her field of intervention, it is *a fortiori* true that that principle is not to be found in the texts of Lenin. She did on occasion articulate differences with him and did address herself to issues which, as revolutionaries, she and he faced in common, so that there is nothing illegitimate in attempting a comparative assessment, although that has not been our aim. But unless it is founded on a prior effort to understand her in her own *specific* context and terms, Luxemburg's meaning invariably suffers. She is treated as though her whole life were one long dialogue with Lenin, or merely an extended endeavour to match what he produced, to give, point for point, as good if not the same. One of the worst variants of this treatment is that which, taking Lenin as the true measure of all things, gauges from Luxemburg's differences with him exclusively her weaknesses and errors. We have no wish to deny his superiority over her, in respects that were decisive, as both revolutionary organiser and theoretician. However, it is well to remember that Lenin was canonised and, as part of that whole process, Luxemburg and others had to be exorcised. The practice, common amongst Leninists and would-be Leninists, of pointing out continually where she fell short of him has by now become tedious if nothing else, and it is more than time to scrutinise her differences with him for what there might be of value on her side. In the nature of things, Luxemburg could not have been Lenin. But the reflection may not be irrelevant that she was also not Zinoviev or Stalin.

It has not, then, been a covert or surreptitious purpose of the arguments in this book to suggest that one can find in Luxemburg's work the equivalent of what is in Lenin's. To say that the old spontaneist-economist charge is baseless and that she well understood the importance of a revolutionary party and leadership, to emphasise the value of the specific strategic conception embodied in her thinking about the mass strike, all of this still does not add up to the distinctively Leninist theory of a revolutionary vanguard organisation, to the sharper sense of the concrete which he brought to this question and to others, to the almost ruthless single-mindedness with which he practised the business of organising a workers' vanguard for the seizure of power. Moreover, there was in her intervention in the dispute between the Bolsheviks and the Mensheviks in 1904 a serious misjudgment of Lenin. However, that is not all there was. There was also a deep and transparent commitment to socialist democracy, one which balked before some of the more unilateral formulations which he allowed himself, in a style of polemic that was always sharp, sometimes excessive and virulent, and destined subsequently to produce by its example some not very happy results. It was that same commitment, in Luxemburg more unequivocal than in most of her contemporaries, that expressed itself in 1918 in certain doubts, worries and reservations about the course of the Russian revolution, at a moment when no one else had time for them. This was not a 'mistake'. It was, as it turned out, a momentous contribution if only for a future revolutionary generation. One can recognise that between the party of Lenin and the triumph of Stalin there is a discontinuity so complete that it had to find a 'biological' expression, in the extermination of the whole generation of old Bolsheviks, that Stalinism is no logical development of Leninism, and so forth – and still say that, in the years following 1918, the Bolshevik party could have used more of such worries as Luxemburg had voiced and a revolutionary of her calibre to fight for them. It would have been slightly less likely, in that event, to have made the mistakes it did which contributed, with more important factors, to the disappearance of soviet democracy. It would have been less likely, at the end of the civil war, to have destroyed the soviet opposition, the Mensheviks and the anarchists, and less likely to have countenanced the prohibition of factions within its ranks. Again, one can recognise that, in the situation that existed in early

1921, the Bolsheviks had no option but to subdue the fortress of Kronstadt – and still say that more of the sensibilities that Luxemburg displayed would have restrained them from the kind of amalgam, transcending the category of 'mistakes', which they made between the sailors and the Whites and which Lukacs merely repeated after them.

To mistakes, in any case, revolutionaries are entitled. But one generation must also learn from those before. The revolutionary left reads Lenin, constantly, assiduously, and so it should. But it does not always have the sense, indeed, the generosity, to identify his mistakes and faults, and to identify them loudly. Proletarian democracy . . . *State and Revolution!* Only, there is no word in there about parties and about the right of different currents to exist within the workers' movement. Today, revolutionaries are not entitled to silence on that question. They must define their attitude towards it. They could begin by reading Rosa Luxemburg.

V

Conclusion

In 1965, in his pursuit of historicist errors, Althusser classi-
fied Rosa Luxemburg as one of a group of 'leftist' thinkers
for whom Marxism was said to be the direct expression of the
proletarian movement rather than a theory imported into it
from outside: 'all the themes of spontaneism rushed into
Marxism through this open breach'. Prominent in the same
group was the name of Karl Korsch. Some three decades
earlier, Korsch had, for his part, identified her and others,
Lenin amongst them, with the opposite error: of having
understood Marxism as precisely something brought to the
workers' movement from outside instead of as that movement's theoretical expression.[1] Recently, on the other hand,
Rossana Rossanda has located in Luxemburg's thought a
conception in which the theory of the class struggle is dependent upon that struggle without being its spontaneous expression, since it can neither be 'assimilated to the immediate
consciousness which the mass has of itself' nor be considered,
as in Lenin's *What is to be done?*, to be 'the pure product of
culture'. All the same, according to Rossanda this position
of hers was 'condemned by the failure of the German and
the European revolution'.[2] Again, Luxemburg's emphasis

[1] See Althusser and Balibar, *op. cit.*, pp. 119–20, 140–1, and Korsch, *op. cit.*,
pp. 101–3.
[2] R. Rossanda, 'Class and Party', in R. Miliband and J. Saville (eds.), *The
Socialist Register 1970*, London 1970, pp. 223–5. Rossanda refers to the following

on both the value of party organisation and its limitations, on the necessity of revolutionary leadership as well as on the creative force of the spontaneity of the masses – this double emphasis is declared by Daniel Guérin to be a 'contradiction'.[3] So it goes. Bertram Wolfe publishes her essay on 'Organisational Questions of Russian Social Democracy' under the title of 'Leninism or Marxism?', on the grounds that the latter is the 'most attractive' title. Robert Conquest delivers himself of the opinion that it was Luxemburg herself who found it 'suitable' to call the essay by that name. Others who know her work better than that, Peter Nettl and *all* of the editors of the three English collections of her political writings, have carelessly asserted that it is Lenin's *What is to be done?* that is the object of Luxemburg's critique in the essay in question.[4]

It is not long ago that there was in certain Marxist quarters an obsession with the question of 'how' to read. We have concluded our treatment of Rosa Luxemburg's ideas with the suggestion that her work is worth reading. But no elaborate metaphysic is required to establish why, if she is to be read to any useful purpose, this task must today be undertaken with a certain elementary care, rigour and respect – which does not of course mean uncritically. The access ways to her thought are already fraught with enough impediments. Some of these are only petty, others larger and more intractable. It is only a bibliographical detail, but English readers coming to her work for the first time through the materials most readily to hand will search in vain in the pages of *What is to be done?* for the formulations with which Luxemburg

passage from *What is to be done?*: 'In the very same way, in Russia, the theoretical doctrine of Social Democracy arose altogether independently of the spontaneous growth of the working class movement; it arose as a natural and inevitable outcome of the development of thought among the revolutionary socialist intelligentsia.' Lenin, *Collected Works*, Vol. 5, pp. 375–6.

[3] D. Guérin, *Rosa Luxemburg et la spontanéité révolutionnaire*, Paris 1971, pp. 39, 42.

[4] See Luxemburg, *The Russian Revolution, and Leninism or Marxism?*, p. 11; R. Conquest, *Lenin*, London 1972, p. 46; Nettl, *op. cit.*, Vol. 1, pp. 286–8; Looker, p. 22; Howard, p. 286 n. 3; Waters, p. 113.

takes issue in her text on organisation. The latter makes no
direct reference to the former but is wholly concerned with
the arguments of *One Step Forward, Two Steps Back*, which
is the actual object of its critique. This point is obviously not
one of world-historical significance, indeed the carelessness
in question is quite understandable, but it is symptomatic
even so. Luxemburg after all was taking issue with *Lenin*,
and on the subject of *the party*, and the relevant *locus classicus*
is *What is to be done?* So what else would she be attacking?
This detail is a symptom, in other words, of a more general
situation in which the specificities of her thought – and these
necessarily include minutiae – are obscured by preconcep-
tions, or sacrificed for the convenience of one or another
polemical purpose. More often than not, the preconception
or the purpose has to do with Luxemburg's views on the
organisation/consciousness of the vanguard in relation to the
spontaneity of the masses. It is just here that the impediments
to understanding are largest and most intractable. For there
is now a mountain of words concurring in the judgment that
she was simply wrong about all this, or well-meaning perhaps
but naive, in any case a 'failure'. As success breeds epigones
so failure encourages a certain kind of licence: in the mountain
of words ostensibly on Rosa Luxemburg's inadequacies there
are many that are connected in only the most tenuous way
to what she actually wrote. Thus, the contradictory positions
attributed to her by Althusser and by Korsch are simply
inverted reflections of their own opposed postures, both
equally unilateral because governed by the common assumption that the relationship of Marxism to the class struggle
must be either one of exteriority or one of expression. But this
polar opposition does not illuminate her thought. To speak
of a complex, or even dialectical, interrelationship between
Marxism and the proletarian movement, between spontaneity
and organisation, may not by itself resolve very much, but
it is a more helpful and more accurate beginning than either
of those two characterisations. It at least prompts one to
look for, and at, the several different sides of the complex
'dialectic' in question. That has been the object of the fore-

going essays.

From her very first entrance into the life and debates of the German socialist movement, Luxemburg was committed to a set of propositions regarding the tendencies of capitalist development that separated her from any spontaneist or organicist conception of the transition to socialism. However paradoxical this may appear, it is nevertheless a fact that her belief in the inevitability of capitalist breakdown was no support for an attitude of fatalist inactivism. For the forms of this breakdown, already beginning to appear on the horizon, were not to be looked upon with complacency. Unchecked, they would lead the working class, and humanity as a whole, to disaster. Luxemburg's vision of capitalist breakdown, sketched during the revisionist controversy, theoretically elaborated later in *The Accumulation of Capital*, a constant presence in her writing in between, was a vision of the convulsive irrationalities with which imperialist capitalism threatened mankind if its progressive achievements were not released by the proletarian revolution. In the absence of the socialist alternative, capitalist collapse meant a slide towards catastrophe – as she came to call it, barbarism. Whatever criticisms can be made of the errors in her economic reasoning, or of the apocalyptic extreme to which she carried this idea, there is no doubt that it gave to her thought a dimension almost entirely lacking in other socialists of her generation, who were dominated to one degree or another by an easy, evolutionist optimism of progress. In the organic laws of capitalism, Luxemburg read the signs of something else, a world of economic stagnation and crisis, of political reaction, of war. A determined fighter for a better world, she nevertheless understood something of the terrible darkness that could and did overtake the new century. That was why the struggle was urgent: Social Democracy had to win the masses for socialism.

Her revolutionary catastrophism did have its negative effects. While it opposed her to the liberal and reformist illusion that everything must automatically continue to get better, it led also to an underestimation of bourgeois democracy's resilience and capacity for integrating the masses, as of the bourgeoisie's loyalty to this type of polity at least where it had acquired, and so long as it retained, that capacity for integration. A corollary of her thesis on the bankruptcy of bourgeois democracy was that the proletariat must save the latter from, and use it against, an increasingly reactionary bourgeoisie. This strategic emphasis, coupled with a mechanical transposition on to Russia of the notion of 'necessary' historical stages, led to the adoption of Luxemburg's perspective for the Russian revolution with its distinctive combination of strength and limitations. Its main strength lay in an acknowledgment that, in Russia – where indeed bourgeois democracy was bound to be still-born and the bankruptcy thesis therefore wholly applicable – any thoroughgoing settlement of accounts with the Tsarist order would require the proletariat to move decisively into struggle and assume the leadership of all the revolutionary forces, even to lay its hands on political power. Luxemburg was not impressed by the argument that such a struggle for power was premature. It was necessary if anything substantial was to be won; and she always maintained, in any case, that the proletariat's seizure of power must, in a sense, inevitably be premature. 'The masses', as she said once, 'must learn how to use power, by using power. There is no other way.'[5] The limitation in her perspective, as in Lenin's, was the dogmatic and paradoxical insistence that this revolutionary struggle of the Russian proletariat would be unable to do more than install a bourgeois-democratic republic, that it could only clear the ground for a further and freer development of Russian capitalism. In the end, the actual dynamic of the Russian revolution in 1917 freed her thinking from this limitation and, in doing so, led to her endorsement of the October Revolution and, with it, of the strategic and programmatic insight which Trotsky had gained from 1905. But, even behind the inadequacy in her conception, there had been a positive impulse. Luxemburg appreciated the vital importance of elementary democratic rights as instruments

[5] 'Speech to the Founding Convention of the German Communist Party', Waters, p. 426.

for the self-emancipation of the working class. It must do all it could to secure, to preserve and to extend them. From classical Marxism and the West she transmitted this kind of emphasis, in the company naturally of the other Marxists of the Russian Empire, into an environment where the Blanquist and populist prejudices of an indigenous tradition stood opposed to it.

Where she thought to detect the same kind of prejudices invading Russian Marxism itself, as she did in Lenin's arguments in 1904, she protested against that too. In 1918 she protested, equally, against what she regarded as a failure of the Bolshevik leadership to weigh fully the dangers that were involved in restricting democratic rights and liberties. This was not the protest of a liberal or an anarchist against the dictatorship of the proletariat, nor an appeal to universal freedom or to interclass democracy against coercion of any kind, nor the plea of a pacifist to the effect that the masses must join battle with an enemy armed to the teeth, shielded only by the strength of their ideals. It was not an idealism of the harmony between means and ends, an idealism which is empty, because impossible to achieve in a material world of complex (or 'over-') determination and, therefore, not respected in practice even by those who articulate it. Nor was Luxemburg criticising the Bolsheviks with the assistance of a theory of organic-economic or unconscious-automatic transition. She was warning them against the temptation to rigidify necessities, that she acknowledged to be largely imposed on them, into some kind of model or principle. They should, on the contrary, recognise unambiguously that the masses needed, in order to work out their own liberation, the fullest possible complement of democratic rights, including the right to support different tendencies/parties, and that insofar as inroads had had to be made on these rights, this was a deformation of the Russian revolution and not a virtue. Only if there was such a recognition could that deformation be corrected in future rather than being made worse. In the light of the subsequent historical development, the judgment that Luxemburg was here mistaken cannot be sustained. She displayed a foresight achieved by none of the Bolshevik leaders in the thick of the struggle. And her concern for democracy in Russia differed from that expressed at this time by other 'socialists' in Europe, by virtue of its clearly revolutionary content.

In fact, amongst the best revolutionary thinkers of her generation, Rosa Luxemburg, was, perhaps, in a uniquely suitable position to represent *to* the workers' movement of Tsarist Russia, a sensitivity over questions of democratic rights where she thought these were being belittled in theory or practice; at the same time, *to* the workers' movement in the West an understanding of, and deep feeling for, the revolutionary vigour, the determination and the bold sweep of mass action, which were so widely decried there. Active in three parties, the German, the Polish and the Russian; deeply interested in, and writing about, the political affairs not only of Russia and Germany, but also of France, of Belgium, of the International as a whole, she spanned some important politico-cultural divisions. Not only that, however, which was true of other Marxists than herself: she had also a capacity and facility for *generalising* the different national experiences for and to one another, for drawing broad lessons from a particular set of events, for taking a long and large view of things. This, it should at once be said, was a source not only of strength. For it meant sometimes that she contributed to the discussion of a concrete problem exclusively generalities. Thus, as Lenin rightly noted in 1904, her critique of *One Step Forward, Two Steps Back* said nothing about the main substance of that work – namely, Lenin's analysis of the situation in the Russian party, of the Second Congress, of the reasons for the split and the refusal of the Mensheviks to respect the decisions of the congress, etc. – but was limited to picking up considerations of a general kind and discussing those.[6] Because of this, Luxemburg ignored the circumstance that, on any meaningful criterion of internal party democracy, it was not Lenin but the Mensheviks who were violating it.

[6] Lenin, *Collected Works*, Vol. 7, pp. 474–8.

Even in this case, however, where Lenin's complaint was entirely justified and her attack on him not, one can detect a difference between her manner of generalising and Lenin's own, which is not wholly in his favour. On the question of internal democracy, for example, Luxemburg offers generalities only, but they leave no doubt as to where she stands. Lenin analyses the present situation – concretely. But in the 'depths' of this concrete situation and in the heat, usually, of a polemic, he also loses sight frequently of the longer and larger view to the extent of *subordinating* the generalisations he makes to the purpose in hand; he speaks as if for all time without always meaning it so. That produces, within the concrete analysis, serious ambiguities. These may be explicable as the consequence of attempts to 'straighten out the stick' and so forth, but this does not render them any more adequate as statements of the problem under discussion.

It is not difficult to find examples: in 1902, Lenin says not only that the broad democratic principle in party organisation is impracticable under conditions of autocratic rule, but also that, given secrecy, and strict selection and training of revolutionaries, 'something even more than "democratism" would be guaranteed to us, namely, complete, comradely, mutual confidence among revolutionaries'; in 1904, 'bureaucracy *versus* democracy is in fact centralism *versus* autonomism; it is the organisational principle of revolutionary Social Democracy as opposed to [that] of opportunist Social Democracy. . . . The former strives to proceed from the top downward, and upholds an extension of the rights and powers of the centre in relation to the parts'; in 1918, 'there is . . . absolutely *no* contradiction in principle between Soviet (*that is*, socialist) democracy and the exercise of dictatorial powers by individuals.'[7] The list could be extended. If Luxemburg's arguments sometimes lacked concreteness they also lacked this sort of thing; and at least part of the reason was the broad comparative scope of her manner of historical generalisation. Where, for instance, in 1904 'bureaucracy-versus-

[7] *ibid.*, Vol. 5, pp. 477–80; Vol. 7, pp. 396–7; Vol. 27, p. 268.

democracy' was for Lenin a polemical way of formulating the need for a unified, centralised and disciplined vanguard party, which could overcome the amateurishness and fragmentation of the Russian movement, she was thinking – already! – of Germany and a danger : the possible conservatism of a powerful, centralised apparatus in the face of mass action and mass militancy.[8] The danger of bureaucratisation was hardly a burning problem of the *Russian* movement at this time, it is true, and that is one measure of Luxemburg against Lenin. On the other hand, the time came when it was. Lenin then completely underestimated the danger until it was too late, too late for him and for the Bolshevik party. That throws a wholly different light on 'bureaucracy-versus-democracy'. It provides also another, complementary measurement of the two revolutionaries.

It was, in any case, from the experience of the Russian movement that Luxemburg began to glean some of the answers to questions posed for her by the German one. The question of how to transcend the dualism of minimum and maximum programmes and to make the 'ultimate' goal of revolutionary proletarian power a real factor in the strategic calculations of Social Democracy, this question, which had exercised her from the time of the revisionist controversy and which was in fact an open question for revolutionary socialism in general, found its first response, under the impact of 1905, in her theory of the mass strike. She saw in the latter the potentialities for linking economic to political demands, political to industrial struggles, the everyday concerns of the masses into a global assault on the capitalist order. She saw there too the necessary conditions for the most widespread implantation of a revolutionary consciousness, as well as the germinal forms of a genuine proletarian democracy. She understood better than any of her contemporaries in this period the preconditions for destroying the bourgeois state. In this connection, Luxemburg registered the importance of spontaneous mass initiatives in creating revolutionary situa-

---

[8] 'Organisational Questions of Russian Social Democracy', Waters, p. 121.

tions and extolled their educative effects. She also pointed to the danger of their being dissipated in the absence of clear direction and conscious leadership. She insisted, therefore, on the indispensability of a revolutionary workers' organisation with an understanding based in Marxism, in a scientific knowledge of bourgeois society, and acting to prepare the ground for the mass struggle. And she pointed to different types of limitation in party organisations: to the inability of even the best of them to conjure up a revolutionary mass upsurge at will and to the danger from others that they might in the end form an obstacle to revolution. Only from an exceedingly unilateral point of view can these be seen as 'contradictions'. Nor is it clear why Luxemburg's position in this matter, with its 'strong link between spontaneity and organisation',[9] should be said to have been condemned by the failure of the European revolution. No doubt that failure raises serious questions about all of the Marxism of that epoch. But after all more than half a century has now elapsed and there is still no socialism in Europe. Why should Rosa Luxemburg's deficiencies have to bear the whole burden of this historical 'delay'? It testifies to the existence of a mass of problems of both theory and practice which the revolutionary socialist movement has yet to resolve. Luxemburg's ideas, a fine product of that movement, will surely provide one starting point.

[9] Rossanda, *loc. cit.*

Bibliography

1. **Writings of Rosa Luxemburg**

Howard, D. (ed.), *Selected Political Writings of Rosa Luxemburg*, New York and London 1971.

Looker, R. (ed.), *Rosa Luxemburg : Selected Political Writings*, London 1972.

Waters, M.-A. (ed.), *Rosa Luxemburg Speaks*, New York 1970.

Note : Of the above three items, the most useful, singly, is the Waters collection, even though it contains old translations which are on the whole rather poor. It is the only one of the three, however, that contains all of 'Social Reform or Revolution', 'Organisational Questions of Russian Social Democracy', 'The Mass Strike, the Political Party and the Trade Unions', 'The Junius Pamphlet', 'The Russian Revolution' and the 'Speech to the Founding Convention of the German Communist Party'. The Looker collection has complete versions of none of these, and the Howard only of the first, second and last. But both of them contain important supplementary material, in better translations, the Howard having in particular three speeches, and a complete version of 'Militia and Militarism', from the period of the revisionist controversy, and the Looker ten pieces from the period of the German revolution as well as an important article on the mass strike, 'The Next Step'. There is a comprehensive bibliography of Luxemburg's works in the biography by J. P. Nettl (q.v.) at pp. 863–917.

Luxemburg, R., *The Russian Revolution & Leninism or Marxism?*, with an introduction by B. D. Wolfe, Ann Arbor 1961.

——, *The Accumulation of Capital*, London 1963.

——, 'The Accumulation of Capital – An Anti-Critique', in Luxemburg, R., and Bukharin, N., *Imperialism and the Accumulation of Capital*, ed. K. Tarbuck, London 1972, pp. 47–150.

——, 'The Second and Third Volumes [of *Capital*]', in Mehring, F., *Karl Marx : The Story of his Life*, London 1936, pp. 370–380.

——, 'The Belgian General Strike of 1902' (five articles), in *Permanent Revolution* (Journal of Workers' Fight), No. 1, Spring 1973, pp. 33–46.

——, *Oeuvres II : Écrits politiques 1917–1918*, Paris 1969.

——, *Lettres à Karl et Luise Kautsky*, Paris 1970.

——, *Lettres à Léon Jogichès*, 2 vols., ed. V. Fay, Paris 1971.

——, 'Blanquisme et social-démocratie', in *Quatrième Internationale*, No. 2, Nouvelle Série, April 1972, pp. 53–55.

——, Speeches to the 1907 congress of the Russian Social-Democratic Party, in *Pyatyi (Londonskii) S"ezd RSDRP, Aprel'-mai 1907 goda, Protokoly*, Moscow 1963, pp. 97–104, 383–92, 432–37.

2. Other Works Cited

Against Trotskyism : A Collection of Documents, Moscow 1972.

Althusser, L., *For Marx*, London 1969.

——, and Balibar, E., *Reading Capital*, London 1970.

Arblaster, A., 'The Relevance of Anarchism', in Miliband, R., and Saville, J. (eds.), *The Socialist Register 1971*, London 1971, pp. 157–84.

——, 'Liberal Values and Socialist Values', in Miliband, R., and Saville, J. (eds.), *The Socialist Register 1972*, London 1972, pp. 83–104.

Arendt, H., 'Rosa Luxemburg: 1871–1919', *Men in Dark Times*, London 1970, pp. 33–56.

Avenas, D., *Économie et politique dans la pensée de Trotsky*, Paris 1970.

Avrich, P., *Kronstadt 1921*, New York 1974.

——, *The Russian Anarchists*, Princeton 1971.

Basmanov, M., *Contemporary Trotskyism : Its Anti-Revolutionary Nature*, Moscow 1972.

Basso, L., 'Rosa Luxemburg: The Dialectical Method', *International Socialist Journal*, No. 16–17, November 1966, pp. 504–41.

——, *Rosa Luxemburg : A Reappraisal*, London 1975.

Bernstein, E., *Evolutionary Socialism*, New York 1961.

Bookchin, M., *Post-Scarcity Anarchism*, London 1974.

The British Road to Socialism, Programme of the Communist Party, London 1968.

Carr, E. H., *The Bolshevik Revolution 1917–23*, 3 vols., Harmondsworth 1966.

——, 'Red Rosa', *1917 : Before and After*, London 1969, pp. 44–57.

Carsten, F. L., 'Freedom and Revolution: Rosa Luxemburg', in Labedz, L. (ed.), *Revisionism*, London 1962, pp. 55–66.

Chossudovsky, M., 'Chicago Economics, Chilean Style', *Monthly Review*, Vol. 26, No. 11, April 1975, pp. 14–17.

Cliff, T., *Rosa Luxemburg*, London 1968.

Cohen, G. A., 'Remarks on Revolutionary Perspectives', *Radical Philosophy*, No. 2, Summer 1972, p. 23.

Colletti, L., *From Rousseau to Lenin*, London 1972.

Conquest, R., *Lenin*, London 1972.

Degras, J. (ed.), *The Communist International 1919–1943*, Documents, Vol. 1, London 1956.

Deutscher, I., *The Prophet Armed*, London 1954.

Eliot, T. S., *Four Quartets*, London 1959.

Engels, F., *Anti-Dühring*, Moscow 1959.

Evans, M., *Karl Marx*, London 1975.

Frölich, P., *Rosa Luxemburg: Ideas in Action*, with a postcript by I. Fetscher, London 1972.

Gay, P., *The Dilemma of Democratic Socialism*, New York 1962.

Geras, N., 'Political Participation in the Revolutionary Thought of Leon Trotsky', in G. Parry (ed.), *Participation in Politics*, Manchester 1972, pp. 151–68.

Guérin, D., *Rosa Luxemburg et la spontanéité révolutionnaire*, Paris 1971.

Huxley, A., *Ends and Means*, London 1937.

Johnstone, M., 'Trotsky: His Ideas', *Cogito* (Journal of the Young Communist League), No. 5, London n.d. (1969?).

Joll, J., *The Second International 1889–1914*, London 1968.

Kautsky, K., *The Class Struggle*, New York 1971.

——, *The Dictatorship of the Proletariat*, Ann Arbor 1964.

——, *The Road to Power*, Chicago 1909.

Korsch, K., *Marxism and Philosophy*, London 1970.

Lee, G., 'Rosa Luxemburg and the Impact of Imperialism', *The Economic Journal*, Vol. 81, No. 324, December 1971, pp. 847–62.

Lenin, V. I., *Collected Works*, 45 vols., Moscow 1960–1970.

Lichtheim, G., 'Rosa Luxemburg', *The Concept of Ideology and Other Essays*, New York 1967, pp. 193–203.

——, *Marxism: An Historical and Critical Study*, London 1964.

Liebman, M., *Leninism Under Lenin*, London 1975.

Lowy, M., *Dialectique et Révolution*, Paris 1973.

——, 'Il significato metodologico della parola d'ordine "socialismo o barbarie"', *Problemi del Socialismo*, 3° serie, anno XIII, no. 1, 1971.

——, *La théorie de la révolution chez le jeune Marx*, Paris 1970.

Lukacs, G., *History and Class Consciousness*, London 1971.

Magri, L., 'Problems of the Marxist Theory of the Revolutionary Party', *New Left Review*, No. 60, March/April 1970, pp. 97–128.

Maitan, L., 'The Theory of Permanent Revolution', in Mandel, E. (ed.), *Fifty Years of World Revolution*, New York 1968, pp. 50–69.

Mandel, E., *The Leninist Theory of Organisation*, London 1971.

——, 'Rosa et la social-démocratie allemande', *Quatrième Internationale*, No. 48, March 1971, pp. 11–20.

Marcuse, H., *Eros and Civilisation*, New York 1961.

Marx, K., *Capital*, 3 vols., Moscow 1961–62.

——, *The Poverty of Philosophy*, Moscow 1966.

——, *Early Writings*, ed. T. B. Bottomore, London 1963.

——, and Engels, F., *Selected Works*, 3 vols., Moscow 1969.

——, and Engels, F., *Selected Correspondence,* Moscow n. d.

Mavrakis, K., *Du Trotskysme,* Paris 1971.

Mehringer, H., 'Introduction historique' to Trotsky, L., *Nos Tâches Politiques,* Paris 1970.

Mills, C. W., *The Marxists,* Harmondsworth 1963.

Morgenstern, C., 'Trotsky et Rosa Luxemburg', *Quatrième Internationale,* No. 48, March 1971, pp. 21–25.

Nettl, J. P., *Rosa Luxemburg,* 2 vols., London 1966.

Rossanda, R., 'Class and Party', in Miliband, R., and Saville, J. (eds.), *The Socialist Register 1970,* London 1970, pp. 217–31.

Schorske, C. E., *German Social Democracy 1905–1917,* New York 1970.

Schurer, H., 'The Russian Revolution of 1905 and the Origins of German Communism', *The Slavonic and East European Review,* Vol. 39, 1960–61, pp. 459–71.

Stalin, J., *Leninism,* London 1940.

——, *Works,* Vol. 13, Moscow 1955.

Stedman Jones, G., 'The Marxism of the Early Lukacs: an Evaluation', *New Left Review,* No. 70, November/December 1971, pp. 27–64.

Sweezy, P. M., *The Present as History,* New York 1953.

——, *The Theory of Capitalist Development,* London 1946.

Trotsky, L., 'Hands Off Rosa Luxemburg!', *Writings of Leon Trotsky 1932,* New York 1973, pp. 131–42.

——, *The History of the Russian Revolution,* 3 vols., London 1932–33.

——, 'The History of the Russian Revolution to Brest-Litovsk', in *The Essential Trotsky,* London 1963, pp. 21–111.

——, 'Luxemburg and the Fourth International', *Writings of Leon Trotsky 1935–36,* New York 1970, pp. 111–12.

——, *My Life,* New York 1960.

——, *1905,* London 1972.

——, *On Britain,* New York 1973.

——, *The Permanent Revolution & Results and Prospects,* London 1962.

——, *The Revolution Betrayed,* New York 1965.

——, *The Struggle Against Fascism in Germany,* New York 1971.

——, *The Transitional Program for Socialist Revolution,* New York 1973.

——, Dewey, J., and Novack, G., *Their Morals and Ours,* Four Essays, New York 1966.

Vollrath, E., 'Rosa Luxemburg's Theory of Revolution', *Social Research,* Vol. 40, No. 1, Spring 1973, pp. 83–109.

Index